TWAYNE'S WORLD AUTHORS SERIES
A Survey of the World's Literature

ITALY

Carlo Golino, University of Massachusetts

EDITOR

Antonio Fogazzaro

TWAS 470

Antonio Fogazzaro

ANTONIO FOGAZZARO

By ROBERT A. HALL, JR.
Cornell University

TWAYNE PUBLISHERS
A DIVISION OF G. K. HALL & CO., BOSTON

Library of Congress Cataloging in Publication Data

Hall, Robert Anderson, 1911 -
    Antonio Fogazzaro.

    (Twayne's world authors series ; TWAS 470 : Italy)
    Bibliography: p. 147 - 52
    Includes index.
    1.   Fogazzaro, Antonio, 1842 - 1911—Criticism and interpreta-
tion.
PQ4688.F6Z873   853'.8   77-22574
ISBN 0-8057-6311-2

To Lucienne Portier

Contents

About the Author

Now Professor Emeritus of Linguistics and Italian at Cornell University, Robert Anderson Hall, Jr. received his A.B. from Princeton and his A.M. from the University of Chicago. He is a Dottore in Léttere from the University of Rome. Although the major part of his career has been spent at Cornell, Professor Hall also taught at Princeton, Brown, and the University of Puerto Rico. His publications relating to Italian language and literature include: *A Short History of Italian Literature* (Ithaca, 1951); *Italian for Modern Living* (Ithaca, 1959), *Italian Short Stories* (New York, 1960), and *La Struttura dell'italiano* (Rome, 1971).

Preface

My intent in this study is to describe and analyze the work of the Italian novelist and poet Antonio Fogazzaro (1842 - 1911). His reputation has been subject to the pendulum-swings of fortune. After a period of disesteem, he is again coming, in the 1970's, to be regarded with critical favor as one of the leading Italian writers of the late nineteenth century whose work deserves attention both in its own right and because of the light it sheds on its times.

Fogazzaro's writings and the development of his views as expressed in them were very closely related to his own personal history. I have therefore devoted my first six chapters to his biography and to the description and discussion of his major works. The remaining three chapters treat his subject-matter and narrative technique, his use of language and music, and his relevance to Italian culture and literature. Since prior acquaintance with his writings cannot be assumed, I have given brief outlines of the contents of each novel and of a few important short stories. For the same reason, I have given brief descriptions of the political and religious situation in late nineteenth-century Italy, a knowledge of which is essential to an understanding of Fogazzaro's works. Where the Italian text is important for an understanding of his style, I have given it together with an English translation; elsewhere, the English alone is quoted.

My prime sources of information for Fogazzaro's life have been the biographies by Gallarati-Scotti, Nardi, and the Piccionis (see the Selected Bibliography). The pioneering study by Lucienne Portier remains the most valuable analysis of Fogazzaro's subject-matter and poetic style. From Giorgio de Rienzo's work on *Fogazzaro and the Experience of Reality,* I have gained increased understanding of Fogazzaro's methods of giving his reader a feeling of having personally lived through the events and known the persons with whom his stories deal.

Italian conventional spelling does not normally indicate the position of stress-accent, except in words where it falls on the last syllable. Dictionaries and grammars, and a few writers, however, do give an indication of the position of stress for all words where it does not fall on the next to the last syllable. Such a procedure is wholly permissible,[1] and I have followed it so as to aid readers in the accurate pronunciation of such words and names as *cémbalo* "harpsichord, piano," *Èlena* "Helen," or the place-name *Rìmini*.

In the hyphenation of English compounds, I have tried to be completely consistent,[2] by using a hyphen in every instance where the first element has full stress and the second has intermediate stress in pronunciation. Dictionaries are, in general, extremely inconsistent in their hyphenation, and readers are needlessly confused thereby. Differences in spoken stress often convey differences in meaning, as between, say, *a Frénch-stùdent* "a student of French" and *a Frénch stúdent* "a student who is French." I therefore hyphenate all compounds like *súbject-màtter, stréss-àccent,* or *pláce-nàme*. The resultant gain in clarity and comprehensibility compensate, I believe, for an unaccustomed consistency.

I have also followed earlier American custom in distinguishing the verb *practise* from the noun *practice;* in writing *in no wise* as three words; and in spelling the verb *analyse* with *s* (in conformity with its derivation from the noun *analysis*).

ROBERT A. HALL, JR.

Cornell University

Chronology

1842   Antonio Fogazzaro is born at Vicenza, March 25.

1856   Enters liceo.

1858   Enrolls in University of Padua law-school.

1860   Moves with family to Turin and continues law-school.

1863   Publishes first poem, *Una ricordanza del Lago di Como*.

1864   Receives law-degree at University of Turin, August.

1865   Family moves to Milan, November.

1866   Marries Margherita di Valmarana, July 31.

1868   Passes bar-examination at Milan, May 20.

1869   Returns with family to Vicenza. Begins *Miranda*. First daughter, Gina, born, July 20.

1870   First plans for *Malombra*.

1871   Gives lecture *Dell'avvenire del romanzo in Italia* to Accademia Olìmpica of Vicenza, May 21; published same year.

1873   Reconversion to Catholic religion, November. Completion of *Miranda*, November.

1874   *Miranda* published, May.

1875   Son, Mariano, born, April 5. Completion of *Valsolda*.

1876   *Valsolda* published. Begins serious work on *Malombra*.

1880   *Malombra* completed, May.

1881   Daughter, Maria, born, February 8. *Malombra* published, May. *Daniele Cortis* begun, May 30. *Un pensiero di Ermes Torranza* written. Felicitas Buchner takes position as governess of Valmarana children, December 1.

1882   *Un'idea di Ermes Torranza* published.

1883   Entry in diary (in English): "Friend, not lover. Never," June 30. Definitive abandonment of love for Felicitas Buchner, July 3. Meets Ellen Starbuck at Lanzo d'Intelvi, August.

1884   *Daniele Cortis* completed, March 11. Uncle Pietro Barrera dies, August. First notes for *Piccolo mondo antico*, August 16.

1885   *Daniele Cortis* published, January. *Fedele* and *Eden Anto* published, March. Trip to Germany, May. *Il fiasco del*

Maestro Chieco published, July. *Il mistero del poeta* begun, November.

1886   *Pereat Rochus* published, January 3. Assumes various minor administrative positions in Vicenza.

1887   *Fedele ed altri racconti* published, January. Father, Mariano, dies, April 11. *Il mistero del poeta* completed, October.

1888   *Il mistero del poeta* published: in installments in *La Nuova Antologia*, January 1 - April 16; in book-form, July.

1889   *Màlgari* published, April 27. Reads Le Conte's *Evolution and its Relation to Religious Thought.*

1891   Gives lecture, *Per un recente raffronto delle teorie di Sant'Agostino e di Darwin*, February 21. Mother dies, April 15.

1892   Gives lecture, *Per la bellezza di un'idea*, May 2.

1893   Gives lecture, *L'origine dell'uomo e il sentimento religioso*, March 2.

1894   *Racconti brevi* published. *Piccolo mondo antico* finished, December 31.

1895   Gives lecture *I misteri dello spirito umano e la scienza*. January 24 and February 2, at Rome. Son Mariano dies, May 16. *Piccolo mondo antico* published, November.

1897   Gives lecture *Le grand poète de l'avenir*, Paris, March 8. Begins *Piccolo mondo moderno*.

1898   *Poesie scelte* and *Discorsi* published.

1899   *Ascensioni umane* published.

1900   *Piccolo mondo moderno* published in installments, December 16, 1900 - March 16, 1901.

1901   *Piccolo mondo moderno* published in book-form, April. *I|dilii spezzati, Minime*, and *El garòfalo rosso* published.

1902   *El garòfalo rosso* and *Il ritratto mascherato* performed, February. *Nadejde* completed, July.

1903   *Il santo* begun.

1905   *Il santo* completed and published, November.

1906   *Il santo* placed on Index, April 4.

1907   Meeting of "modernists" at Molveno, August. Encyclical *Pascendi* published, September 8.

1908   *Le poesie* published, November 12.

1909   *Leila* begun.

1910   *Leila* completed, May 25; published, November 12.

1911   Fogazzaro dies at Vicenza, March 7. *Leila* placed on Index, May 8.

CHAPTER 1

A Slow Start

I Earliest Upbringing

ANTONIO Fogazzaro was born in Vicenza, a city of northern Italy, on March 25, 1842, the son of Mariano Fogazzaro and Teresa Barrera. On his father's side, he was descended from a commercial family of ultimately humble origin. Coming from a village (Cuntrà Fugazzari) near the small Venetian town of Schio, they had become well-to-do through trading in wool. Antonio's grandfather, Giovanni Antonio Fogazzaro, had moved from Bèrgamo to Vicenza where he acquired a city house and a farm at nearby Montegalda. Giovanni Antonio was authoritarian, conservative, and not highly cultured. His children, on the contrary, were liberal in politics, deeply religious, and interested in cultural matters.

Three of Mariano's brothers and sisters exercised an especially strong influence on the young Antonio's development. His aunt Maria Innocente was a nun of the Salesian order, given to acute inner psychological conflicts and mystical experiences. His two uncles, Luigi (Gigio) and Giuseppe, also never married. Luigi was a landed proprietor whom Antonio often visited as a boy at Montegalda, and of whom he was especially fond because of his uncle's cheerfulness, sense of humor, and love of good living. Giuseppe, on the other hand, was a priest with extensive intellectual interests and curiosity, and strongly liberal in political sympathies. Don Giuseppe[1] was a great admirer of the liberal Catholic philosopher Rosmini.[2]

Antonio's mother was of peasant stock from Oria, a village on Lake Lugano, in the region known as Valsolda, just east of the border between Switzerland and Italy. Her father was an architect who had moved to Milan and thence to Vicenza where she met and married Mariano Fogazzaro. Teresa was six years older than Mariano, with a somewhat firmer character than her intellectually

13

able but dreamy, poetical, and musical husband. The marriage was contrary to the wishes of Mariano's father; the young couple lived at first with Teresa's parents, and were helped financially by Teresa's uncle, Pietro Barrera, an engineer from Como. Antonio had two siblings, an older brother named Carlo, who died in childhood, and a younger sister Innocentina (Ina).

Antonio's earliest years coincided with the middle period of the movement known as the Risorgimento, or "resurgence" of a united Italy, which lasted altogether from 1815 to 1870. His father took part in the defense of Verona against the Austrian troops in the uprising of May and June, 1848;[3] his uncle Don Giuseppe was active as both a soldier and a civilian administrator during the conflict.[4] As a school-boy, Antonio read extensively in Italian and learned French and Latin well. For two years (1856 - 58) he was a student in the *liceo* (roughly equivalent to our senior high school), where his chief teacher was the poet-priest Zanella.[5] From Zanella, the adolescent Fogazzaro learned to love the romantic aspects of Vergil and of German poetry, especially Heine (whom Antonio first read in a French translation). Later, he acquired a thorough knowledge of both German and English, in which latter language he frequently read the Bible.

At this stage, Antonio already felt the urge to become a poet, but Mariano (like so many fathers in similar situations) wished to see his son enter the more lucrative profession of law. Somewhat unwillingly, therefore, Antonio enrolled as a law-student at the University of Padua in 1858. Poor health and the disturbed conditions of the times kept him from pursuing his studies continuously or effectively. Much of 1859 was spent at Oria and elsewhere in accordance with his family's habit—which he kept up throughout his lifetime—of frequent travel. In this way, Valsolda became for him virtually a second home, and the source of much of his poetical inspiration. During this period, Antonio read extensively, wrote much poetry, and became acquainted with a great deal of music (especially German), principally through his father's excellent playing. He himself became a moderately good pianist, but never progressed beyond the amateur level.

II   *Law versus Poetry*

By mid-1860, peace had returned to northern Italy. Lombardy was joined to Piedmont, but Venetia was still under Austrian rule.

Mariano was determined not to return to Vicenza until it had been liberated and united to Italy. He renewed his insistence that Antonio continue his law-studies, this time at Turin. "Toni" yielded again, but only after a certain amount of resistance. The family therefore moved to Turin, living modestly and making financial sacrifices to enable him to attend the university. Antonio, however, devoted more time to amusements and dissipation than to academic work. To a large extent, this "dissipation" was relatively innocent—mostly playing billiards and sauntering around town eyeing the girls. He yielded to sexual temptation only once, losing his virginity but being profoundly disgusted by the experience and never again indulging in promiscuous relations.[6]

Antonio's religion also suffered during this period. His family was rigorously orthodox, and he continued the outward practices of the Catholic religion so as not to displease them. Inwardly, however, he turned first to a kind of pantheism and then to an attitude of skepticism, which he did not abandon until over a decade later. For a time, aesthetic sensitivity and poetic expression took the place of religious faith. In politics, on the other hand, he continued, with virtually no interruption, to be a strong monarchist, regarding the House of Savoy as the only centre around which a firmly united Italy could be built.

Mariano's insistence on his son's studying law was largely founded on the poor opinion he had of Antonio's poetical efforts, which he considered dilettantish and inferior. *Una ricordanza del lago di Como* ("A Memory of Lake Como"), written in 1860, is generally regarded as the best of the young Fogazzaro's early productions. It was his first published work, appearing in 1863. Other, very minor poems appeared at irregular intervals during the following years. Both as a poet and as a story-teller, Fogazzaro was a slow starter, at least in part because of his lack of self-confidence, but also because of his perfectionism, which led him to rework his material over and over again.

The entire four years Antonio spent in Turin were, in fact, marked by an over-all disorientation and inability to come to a firm decision concerning his goals in life. He travelled extensively in northern Italy, as far as Genoa, Pisa, and Florence, and of course spent several months every year in Valsolda. Nevertheless, he finally did obtain his law-degree, after a fashion, in 1864. The following year was spent largely in the law-office of a friend of Mariano's.

In November of 1864, Mariano decided to move his family to

Milan. Even in the mid-nineteenth century, Milan was the most cosmopolitan city of northern Italy, with a greater range of cultural attractions and stimulating society than even Turin, to say nothing of smaller, staid provincial centers like Vicenza. For Antonio, this meant opportunities to hear many operas and much other music, and to meet interesting people. Among his friends was the eccentric cellist Gaetano Braga, whom he later portrayed as Maestro Chieco in the short story "Il fiasco del Maestro Chieco" ("Maestro Chieco's fiasco") and in *Piccolo mondo moderno* ("Little World of Nowadays"), and an old revolutionary, Abbondio Chialiva, whom he introduced into *Malombra* as Count Césare d'Ormengo. To one of his best friends of later years, the poet-composer Boito,[7] he was probably not very close at this time, as can be deduced from his strong disapproval of Boito's *Mefistofele* at its *première* on March 5, 1868.

Since childhood, Antonio had been acquainted with the Vicentine family of Count Àngelo Valmarana, including his son Gaetano and his daughter Margherita. In the 1860's, Antonio and Rita met a number of times, and in the early months of 1866 the two became engaged. They were married at Vicenza on July 31, 1866, only two weeks after the city had been liberated from the Austrians. After a honeymoon trip, the newly-weds returned to Milan, where Antonio was—at least in theory—studying for his bar-examinations.

In actuality, young Fogazzaro was still disoriented and deeply discontented. Of those times, he later wrote "I was doing nothing, because my ideals had fallen, and I no longer hoped for anything in life."[8] He was, if not indigent, at least hard up, and Rita did not wholly fulfill his expectations and hopes for a wife sympathetic to poetry and music. Nevertheless, he was then and always remained a completely faithful husband. He worked fitfully at his legal studies, but devoted his major energies to writing poetry. It was not until 1868 that he buckled down in earnest to preparing for the bar-examinations, which he passed on May twentieth of that year. He was now the *avvocato* Antonio Fogazzaro, but was even less interested in exercising his profession than before.

In the following year, 1869, Antonio and Rita moved back to Vicenza where they settled permanently—though not without numerous trips to the Valmarana family estate at Velo d'Àstico (near Vicenza), to Montegalda, to the Little Saint Bernard in Switzerland, and of course to Oria. Their union was blessed with a daughter, Gina, born on July twentieth of that year. During this period, in view of Antonio's continued refusal to practise law, his father tried unsuccessfully to interest him in some other "practical" and lucrative activity, such as teaching political economy. Antonio continued, however, to reject all careers except that of a poet—living, in the meanwhile, on the incomes of the Fogazzaro and the Valmarana families.

The first signs of a break in the impasse came in the early 1870's, when Antonio began to furnish concrete evidence that he possessed true ability as a poet. Perhaps as early as 1869, in addition to writing individual poems, he planned a longer narrative work in verse, *Miranda*. The writing of *Miranda* was one of his major occupations during 1872 and 1873; he completed it in November of the latter year. After Antonio had tried unsuccessfully to interest several publishers, Mariano—suddenly, after reading *Miranda*, converted to a belief in his son's poetic vocation—subsidized its publication, and it appeared in May, 1874. It was received for the most part favorably—more, perhaps, by the reading public than by the critics—but in any case enough so that it was eventually translated into four foreign languages and went into twenty-four editions.[9] Since *Miranda* is essentially a novel, though in verse, it will be discussed in the next chapter.

In these same years, Fogazzaro was also working on two other projects. His attention was beginning to turn to the prose novel, as shown by a lecture *Dell'avvenire del romanzo in Italia* ("On the Future of the Novel in Italy"), given in Vicenza on May 21, 1872, and published in the same year. In this essay, he urges Italian novelists to devote their attention to serious topics, and to replace, in a fully Italian society, the frivolous literature imported from abroad or imitated from foreign (especially French) sources. At the same time, Fogazzaro wrote the opening pages of his first prose novel, *Molombra* (see Chapter 2). Typically, he then allowed this work to lie fallow for several years, while completing *Miranda* and *Valsolda*.

The last-mentioned was a collection of his poems, which he worked into publishable form after the completion of *Miranda* and his reconversion to the inner substance of the Catholic faith. This took place in November, 1873, near the monastery of Praglia, in the Euganean Hills, after Fogazzaro had been reading *La Philosophie du Crédo* ("The Philosophy of the Creed"), by Auguste-Alphonse Gratry. Undoubtedly this was but the final step of a much longer inner process of self-criticism and revision of his religious beliefs.

From this point onwards, his adherence to what he regarded as the essentials of Catholic doctrine was complete and unshakable, as was his belief that the teachings of Christianity should be applied in both private and public life. His newly rediscovered faith is evident also in some of the lyrics of *Valsolda*, which he completed in 1875—the same year in which his greatly longed-for son Mariano was born on April 5—and published in 1876.

Valsolda is a collection of twenty-one lyric poems, of which several are subdivided, notably the last, *Novissima Verba* ("Last Words"), consisting of eleven short sections. All of the poems deal with the region of Valsolda itself, in and around Oria, as perceived by the poet. The great majority are concerned with natural phenomena, viewed either in themselves or in relation to the humans who move in and among them. The poet himself expresses his feelings, not as reflected in nature— in accordance with the now out-worn "pathetic fallacy"—but as they are aroused by and are consonant with nature. Thus, in *Il poeta e la rupe* ("The Poet and the Cliff"), Fogazzaro gives us a conversation between himself and the cliff, with obvious symbolism referring to human aspirations:

Il poeta
Guglia che obliqua rompi nel cielo,
Dimmi il tuo sdegno, se puoi! Non vedi
In giro i verdi monti, ai tuoi piedi
Rider i clivi
Di viti, ulivi,
Scherzar de l'acque l'azzurro velo?
Di là dall'altre vette, giammai,
Guglia, non guardi
Brillar il franto speglio de' gai
Laghi lombardi?

La rupe
A me che importa di verdi monti,
Di laghi sparsi per gli orizzonti,
E di vigneti
E d'oliveti?
La folla io guardo spettrale dei bianchi
Giganti ritti nel Sole ancora
Quando la notte me disnora.
Sento la gloria de' padri miei,
A paro ascendere
Di lor vorrei!

Il poeta

O rupe, t'amo!

La rupe

Se sai, esaltami!

"[The poet:] O pinnacle, rising slanting towards the heavens, explain to me your scorn, if you can! Do you not see the green mountains round about, [and] the slopes at your feet smiling with vines [and] olive-trees, [and] the blue veil of the waters playing? Beyond the other summits, do you never, o pinnacle, look at the broken mirror of the gay Lombard lakes sparkling? [The cliff:] What do I care about green mountains, about lakes scattered along the horizons, and about vineyards and olive-groves? I look towards the ghostly crowd of white giants still erect in the sun when night robs me of honor. I feel the glory of my fathers, [and] I should like to ascend to equal them! [The poet:] O cliff, I love you! [The cliff:] If you can, extol me!"

As has been pointed out,[10] the environment of Valsolda was crucial in forming the young Fogazzaro's attitudes towards nature and natural phenomena. The scale of the terrain and of human living in Valsolda is small, but with a view of the outside world afforded (as suggested in the poem just cited) by both the lake below and the summits of the Alps above. In his childhood, adolescence, and maturity Fogazzaro became intimately acquainted with the physical features and with the flora and fauna of the region. Through this close first-hand knowledge of nature, he was especially enabled to feel the life in animate beings, and to interpret inanimate things as if they were living. Although not a botanist, Fogazzaro knew the individual species of plants in great detail, and introduced them into, not only *Valsolda*, but virtually all his later work. Not that he was doing so as an affectation or to display his erudition: their significance for him was simple and direct, so that it came naturally to him to treat them as immediate symbols of his emotions.

The region of Valsolda itself combines three elements which are fundamental to Fogazzaro's poetical expression: the mountains, the skies, and the lake with its tributary streams.[11] In such a situation, humans are small by comparison, but not overwhelmed. In Fogazzaro's time (and even today, comparatively speaking), Valsolda was quiet, peaceful, and an ideal spot for withdrawal and reflection. At the same time, it was complex enough to offer the poet a whole microcosm, in contemplation of which he could develop and analyse his inner development and his relation to God, the world of nature, and his fellow humans. Even without the "little worlds" explicitly mentioned in the titles of his novels *Piccolo mondo antico* ("Little World of Yesteryear") and *Piccolo mondo moderno,* it would be impossible to escape the conclusion, which many critics have reached,[12] that Fogazzaro's strength as a story-teller lies in his ability to depict limited environments and small groups of humans in close contact with and intense reaction to each other and nature—and that this strength derived above all from his close contact with the "little world" of Valsolda.

In the final poem of *Valsolda* (Number XI of "Novissima Verba"), Fogazzaro urges himself to go out into the world and to fight for the truth and revivified poetry. The last stanza is, as it were, his battle-cry:

> Fra gli uomini! Al fragor d'una lontana
> Battaglia vo per tenebre deserte,
> Pensoso, in arme. Ove si pugna, un posto
> Serbato m'è. Per ogni altera fede
> Che più dal fango imperioso affranca,
> Per ogni forte amor, per ogni sdegno
> Che si accendon da lei, soldato! avanti!

"Among men! To the clash of a distant battle I go through deserted shadows, thoughtful, in arms. Where there is fighting, a place is reserved for me. For every lofty faith which frees [men] from imperious mire, for every strong love, for every noble scorn which catches fire from it, soldier, advance!"

It is not hard to see in this exhortation to himself the expression of Fogazzaro's intent to devote his future literary activities to the causes which he held most dear, especially his newly reaffirmed religious faith and his poetical vocation. He had already begun the battle in *Miranda,* and was soon to continue it in his first major prose work, *Malombra.* His years of indecision and hesitation were over.

CHAPTER 2

The Poet and His Culture

I Miranda

T HE novel-in-verse was a favorite form of narrative in the eighteenth and nineteenth centuries. In Germany, the idyll *Luise* (1784) of Johann Heinrich Voss, and Goethe's *Hermann und Dorothea* (1798) had set the style of idyllic-dramatic stories related in poetry which might vary from the lyric to the epic vein. In England, Sir Walter Scott's *Marmion* (1808) and *The Lady of the Lake* (1810) served as further examples, and the Italian Giovanni Berchet (1783 - 1851) had contributed a major work to the genre in his *I pròfughi di Parga* ("The Refugees from Parga," 1821). Later instances of the same type of narrative poem were Longfellow's *Hiawatha* (1855) and *Evangeline* (1877); Tennyson's *Idylls of the King* (1859 - 1885); and Frédéri Mistral's Provençal idyll *Mirèio* (1859). Fogazzaro's *Miranda* was a worthy continuator of this tradition.

The theme of *Miranda* is quite simple: a young man rejects a girl's love; the girl is unhappy; the young man repents and returns to avow his love for her, but the girl dies. The poem is divided into four parts, which have been compared[1] to the four movements of a sonata. The first, relatively short section, "La Léttera" ("The Letter"), sets forth the situation: in a small village in the Italian Alps, an eighteen-year-old girl, Miranda, lives with her widowed mother and is in love with the nephew of the village doctor. At first this lad, Enrico, is in love with her, but neither of the two makes a declaration of love to the other. Enrico feels the urge to become a writer so strongly that he wishes to devote his life to poetry, but in a purely selfish and histrionic way. He feels offended because Miranda seems indifferent to his poetry. Enrico's uncle and Miranda's mother wish to arrange a marriage between the pair, but Enrico will have none of it, and leaves the village to go to the city. He leaves a

21

letter for Miranda in which he explains that his "vocation" calls him to broader horizons and richer experiences. The second part, "Il libro di Enrico" ("The Book of Enrico") consists of two sections, in the first of which Enrico tells his feelings towards Miranda, and the second his experiences in the city, with its unbridled pursuit of material pleasure. He loses his faith in God, and feels at best a vague pantheistic love of nature.

In "Il libro di Miranda" ("The Book of Miranda"), the third part, she describes her resignation and her growing unhappiness during the following four years. She makes visits to the city (presumably Milan) and to such resorts as the beach at Pisa. She meets a young Englishwoman, Diana, whom Enrico has already known in the city, and she tries unsuccessfully to take part in mundane recreations. Miranda eventually returns to the village to live in loneliness and misery, with her health undermined by progressively worsening heart-disease. She prays to God in her wretchedness that her life may be sacrificed for Enrico's, so that he may live and be redeemed. In the Epilogue (told in the third person), Enrico returns to the village, in part because his uncle is mortally ill, but also because he is disillusioned and weary of self-centered bohemianism. Miranda's prayer has been answered, and her spirit has rescued him, even at a distance.[2] Finally Enrico confesses his love to Miranda, but the shock is too great for her. She suffers a heart-attack on hearing his declaration, and dies. Enrico finally realizes his responsibility for the unhappy outcome of their love. Several times in the course of the poem, the expression *da te, da te solo* "by thee, by thee alone" recurs, and it is repeated in the last stanza, in which Fogazzaro apostrophizes Enrico, telling him that Miranda's heart has been broken *da te, da te solo.*

Versified narrations have fallen out of favor in the century since *Miranda* was published, especially because, in both Italian and English, the metrical form seems unfitted for the freer type of presentation which is now preferred, and the vocabulary and even some grammatical forms seem affected and stilted. In its day, *Miranda* aroused a strong emotional response in its readers; nowadays, it is rarely read except by devout Fogazzarians. This neglect is also due, at least in part, to the very reason which made it popular in its time: it was too close to the spirit of the period. Both women and men were suffering from the inevitable let-down which follows a period of psychological exaltation—in this case the efforts of the Risorgimento, which were finally crowned with success in the unification of Italy in 1870. The ladies liked to think of themselves as pale, sickly, neglected creatures. The men—at least the poets—no longer had the lofty ideals of national liberation to inspire them. Some of the wilder spirits among the men of letters indulged in undisciplined living, for instance the group known as the *Scapigliati* (literally, the "dishevelled ones") in Milan in the 1870's.[3]

Miranda is important, however, in any consideration of Fogazzaro's work because of its relation to his later work and its cultural symbolism. In *Miranda*, almost all the major characteristics of Fogazzaro's more mature work are present. In his portrayal of character, Fogazzaro customarily drew upon his observation of individuals whome he had known, and tended to transpose them bodily into the personages of his stories—though of course combining, to a certain extent, the physical or psychological features of one person with those of another.[4] The individual on whose experiences he drew most was, naturally, himself: the heroes of his novels often embody various facets of Fogazzaro's own personality and outlook. Enrico is clearly, to a large extent, modelled upon the self that Fogazzaro had just overcome being—a young man with a strong sense of his poetical vocation, but excessively self-centered, irreligious, and at the same time uncertain and vacillating. The Englishwoman Diana reflects Fogazzaro's contacts with foreign ladies in Milan and at such resorts as the Little Saint Bernard. Miranda, on the other hand, is rather more of an abstraction, the nineteenth-century ideal of innocent, suffering, patient girlhood, reminiscent of Griselda in mediaeval literature and Boccaccio's *Decameron*.

During his period of alienation from religion, Fogazzaro had dabbled to a certain extent in occultism. After his reconversion to complete faith in 1873, his outlook on life was and remained thoroughly dualistic, with a firm belief in the existence of an incorporal soul separate from the body and the world of the senses. His interest in occultism did not, however, disappear immediately. It is reflected to a certain extent in *Miranda* (the effect on one spirit upon another at a distance through a kind of mental telepathy) and more extensively, as we shall see, in *Malombra*. In *Miranda*, Enrico's experiences clearly symbolize the deceptive appeal of the material world with which the poet becomes disillusioned as opposed to the pure spirituality represented by Miranda.

From the very beginning of *Miranda*, nature and natural

phenomena furnish the background against which the action takes place:

> Alla meridiana ôra di maggio
> Sotto limpidi ciel movonsi pioppi
> Tremoli e le distese praterie.
> Chi sino ai campi che l'aratro inverte
> Non crede unito il mar della verzura?
> Pure tra i fiori e l'erbe occulti rivi
> Parton l'ime radici. In fondo ai prati,
> D'ingenti olmi difesa il tergo e l'ali,
> Siede una casa candida.

"Under the noon-day breeze in May, under a clear sky, move trembling poplars and the wide-stretching fields. Who would not believe that the sea of greenery was not united up to the fields which the plow turns over? Yet among the flowers and the grasses, hidden streams separate the deepest roots. At the bottom of the fields, protected on its back and sides by giant elms, sits a white house." (Note the symbolism of the hidden split in the forest, which is to be the main theme of the poem as applied to the humans who live in the countryside.)

In *Miranda*, we already find Fogazzaro's love of introducing his favorite trees (in this passage, poplars and elms) and plants into his tales. Features of certain specific settings of which he was fond are transferred into his stories: here, the cypress and the wisteria are those which grew beside the Villa Valmarana at Seghe di Velo. The trees and landscapes are intertwined with the characters' emotions, as when Miranda says ("Il libro di Miranda", XXXII):

> A me venia de' monti miei, de' prati
> Solitarii, de' vecchi olmi fedeli
> Una indicibil tenerezza in mente.

"There came into my mind an inexpressible longing for my mountains, for my solitary fields, for the faithful old elms."

Music, also, forms an essential part of the story, reflecting the moods of the characters, especially Miranda, who is an accomplished pianist. In the first scene of the poem, she plays for her mother and Enrico's uncle the doctor, first from printed music and then improvising:

> Ed una giovinetta lenta lenta,
> Pensosa in volto, al cembalo venia,
> Correva e ricorrea da un capo all'altro
> I fragorosi tasti. [. . .] le note
> Ricominciâro furïosamente.
> Le si oscurava il libro, a lor talento
> Vagavano le man' per un pensiero
> Che sùbito la prese.

"And a young woman came, very slowly, with a pensive expression, to the piano; she ran up and down the resounding keyboard from one end to the other. [. . .] the notes began again furiously. The book [of music] grew dark before her eyes; her hands wandered at will, on account of a thought that suddenly seized her." Here the musical activity is central to the action, casting light on Miranda's character (slow, dreamy, inclined to lose awareness of the outside world and to let her thoughts roam, her fingers expressing them as she improvises) and also setting the tone of emotional excitement. In other passages, Fogazzaro describes the effect that Miranda's playing produces. Enrico tells ("Il libro d'Enrico", IX) how powerfully he was affected, but did not dare to utter the praise he felt she deserved. In "Il libro di Miranda," the heroine tells (IX) how she had formerly regarded German music as barbaric, but had come to feel limitless religiosity in it; later in the same book (LXIII), she feels psychological strength coming to her from playing a Neapolitan tarantella set by some German composer (perhaps Liszt).

The only major element of Fogazzaro's writings absent from *Miranda* is humor. Even in *Valsolda*, he has at least one humorous poem, the description (IX, "Don Tomaso") of a dialogue between a fish and a priest who has shamefully neglected his flock. But in *Miranda* the atmosphere is very serious in keeping with Fogazzaro's ultra-romantic approach. In almost all his later fiction, however, his strong sense of humor is never far from the surface.

Miranda is also important in it, at the beginning of his career as a story-teller, Fogazzaro indicated symbolically his attitude towards the relation of the artist (especially the bellettristic writer) to his own culture.[5] Enrico represents the poet, and Miranda symbolizes the culture and mode of life of the village. Enrico finds that when he has rejected the culture with which he has grown up, his refusal to grant it his affection has destroyed it and has at the same time harmed him, so that he remains with nothing at the end. From this point of view, *Miranda* is a *novela ejemplar*, a cautionary tale, in which Fogazzaro is warning young poets not to imitate Enrico's mistake of abandoning their own culture—even if it is that of a small village—for a foreign, false, harmful bohemianism (like that of the Milanese *Scapigliati*) which embodies an erroneous, superficial view of the poet as a self-centered, strutting exhibitionist. At the same time, Fogazzaro suggests to the bearers of "home-town" cultures that they should not be indifferent to the talents of their native artists. In his own life, Fogazzaro always showed appreciation for the culture in which he had been born and raised, and from which he drew his greatest inspiration. There still remained, however, especially for the Italian writer, the problem of his relation to the past, and it is this concern which is symbolized in Fogazzaro's first major work of prose fiction, *Malombra*.

II   Malombra

After finishing *Valsolda*, Fogazzaro got down to work in earnest on *Malombra* in 1876. He never was, at best, a fast worker, and he was slowed down even more by the manifold daily concerns of his household, his growing children, and his frequent trips from Vicenza to nearby or more distant vacation-places. It took him until May of 1880 to complete *Malombra*, and another year passed until it finally appeared in May of 1881. As with his two preceding books, *Malombra* had to be subsidized before a publisher would accept it. Unlike them, it was immediately successful. It was acclaimed by both critics and the reading public, and established Fogazzaro as one of Italy's leading novelists.

The story of *Malombra* is fairly complicated. A young Milanese novelist, Corrado Silla, has been invited by Count Césare d'Ormengo to visit the latter's palace on a lake north of Milan. He is met by the Count's secretary, a German liberal refugee named Andreas Steinegge. They hear the wild piano-playing of the Count's niece, Marina di Malombra, against whom Steinegge warns Silla. The Count turns out to have been an old friend of Silla's mother, and asks Silla to stay and help him write a book. For economic reasons, his niece has had to leave the brilliant society of Paris and to live on her uncle's hospitality in his lonely palace far from all her pleasures. She hates the Count, and spends her time reading novels and—knowing that he hates music—playing operatic excerpts on the piano, especially themes from Meyerbeer's wildly romantic

Robert le Diable. She also has a boat in which she likes to go for solitary rides on the lake, especially to a mysterious *òrrido* or grotto on the opposite shore.

Marina is at first contemptuous of Silla, but her strangely fascinating personality both attracts and repels him. She discovers that he is the author of a book which deals with metempsychosis, published anonymously with the title *Il sogno* ("The Dream"). She reveals to Silla that they have already corresponded, since she has written to the author of *Il sogno* under the pseudonym of "Cecilia" and he has replied. This pseudonym was the given name of an ancestor of Marina's, Cecilia Varrega, who was imprisoned in a room of the palace and so maltreated by her jealous husband, an Ormengo, that she died. Marina has discovered, in a secret drawer of Cecilia's desk, a letter from Cecilia urging the girl in whom she expects to be reïncarnated to avenge her on the Ormengo family. Marina is convinced that she is the reïncarnation of Cecilia, and that Silla embodies the soul of Cecilia's lover.

Silla becomes enamored of Marina, who shows affection for him, while at the same time her hatred of Ormengo grows. A young Venetian, Nepo Salvador, visits the palace together with his family to ask for Marina's hand in marriage. She pretends to encourage them in order to shame the Count in the end by a haughty refusal. Steinegge's long-lost daughter, Edith, a pure, angelic creature, joins him. Steinegge, Edith, and Silla become friendly with the local priest, Don Innocenzo, whose high-minded spirituality they admire. Edith falls secretly in love with Silla, but is distressed at her father's loss of his faith. She prays that Steinegge may recover it, and vows to sacrifice all earthly happiness if this comes to pass. Silla is torn between the physical attraction he feels for Marina, and the spiritual love which Edith arouses in him.

The three leave the palace and go to Milan, where, however, Silla is disgusted with the superficiality of the pretentious, empty upper bourgeois society. After a time, Silla, Steinegge, and Edith return to the palace, at a time when the old Count is seriously ill. Marina carries out her vengeance on Count d'Ormengo by appearing in his bed-room at night and announcing that she is Cecilia's reïncarnation and avenger. The Count dies of shock. Realizing that Silla loves Edith, Marina's love for him turns to a mad hatred, and she shoots him dead. She then eludes pursuit, leaps into her boat, and flees to the other side of the lake, disappearing in the *òrrido*.

This very abbreviated outline gives no idea of the wealth of detail with which Fogazzaro describes scenes and characters, nor of the large number of minor personages, such as the local doctor, the servant-boy Rico (who is secretly and hopelessly enamored of Marina), and of a host of others. The characters may range from uncouth (like Nepo's relatives) to polished (the high-society ladies in Milan), or from imperious, rude, but kindly (the Count) to sweet and self-sacrificing (Edith). One of Fogazzaro's chief merits is his ability to portray his characters, whether major or minor, in different lights as the story proceeds. Steinegge, for instance, at first appears as a likeable, but comic old man (Fogazzaro describes his face as "ugly and cheerful, ridiculous and intelligent, sparkling with life") talking broken Italian as he expounds his liberal, agnostic philosophy to Silla. Later, his depth of character is revealed in his love for his daughter and his awkward but pathetic and touching prayer for her well-being (Part II, Chapter III):

I don't know you well, Lord God, but my Edith loves you and I can worship you, if you wish. You see, I kneel down, but let's reach an understanding between us and leave the priests out of it. Perhaps I can tell you a few other things. I have my health, which is of bronze. Take it. Make me die gradually, but don't come between Edith and me. I can't kneel before priests and lie. I am faithful, I am a soldier. Lord God—here Steinegge knelt on the other knee also and lowered his voice—I fear I sinned a great deal in my youth. I loved gaming and women, the worst ones. Three times, out of the twelve I fought a duel, I was the offender, I wounded the other man, and I was the one who was in the wrong. I believe that these were three sins; I have always had them on my heart. Lord God of my Edith, I beg your forgiveness.

Similarly, the setting of *Malombra* is rich and varied. It includes a number of the stock features of romantic novels: an old palace in the countryside with a small village and church nearby; a thick forest; a somber, gloomy lake, with an awe-inspiring grotto in its rugged bank; and forbidding mountains in the background. But Fogazzaro describes them in such great detail, fitting all the parts of his description together so minutely and skilfully, that the reader accepts them as completely real in the course of his reading. Only after he has finished an entire episode or the whole novel does he realize the extent to which he has been carried along on an over-all wave of suspense with strong over-tones of romantic mystery. In this respect, Fogazzaro's technique is similar to that of Sir Walter

Scott in such a novel as *St. Ronan's Well* (1824), which is both contemporary and "Gothic."

At the same time, Fogazzaro goes far beyond the procedure of those "realistic" or "naturalistic" authors who eschew all description of the thoughts or feelings of their personages. He relates, often in considerable detail, his characters' inner thoughts, wherever they are relevant to the reader's understanding of the situation or the development of the plot. Thus, when Marina has just arrived at Césare d'Ormengo's palace, she looks out into the dark:

> Marina had the shutters opened and threw herself on the sill of a window, thrusting her head into the dark, into the wind, into the mixed crashing of the waves and the woods, all of them voices of reproof and of threats which seemed to her to be friends of the irritable Count—full, at one and the same time, of a superior and wicked power.

Here, as in many other passages, Fogazzaro first portrays a scene and then describes the effect it has on one or more characters. His technique combines realism, in the best sense of the term—exact, detailed description of settings and persons—with perceptive psychological analysis.

The autobiographical element in *Malombra* is perhaps greater than in any of Fogazzaro's later novels except *Il mistero del poeta* ("The Mystery of the Poet"). Both Silla and Marina reflect their creator's earlier interest in occultism, especially metempsychosis. Before the story begins, they have both had this interest to about the same degree; but in the course of the novel, their relation to the subject develops in different directions. Silla is at first attracted to Marina, to a considerable extent, because of this common interest. As she becomes more and more unbalanced in her belief that she is Cecilia Varrega reïncarnated, Silla comes to perceive the harmful nature of her obsession. He is on the way to abandoning his skepticism and irreligion (which reminds us, of course, of Enrico in *Miranda*), and to acquiring spiritual calm and strength through his nascent love for Edith when Marina, infuriated by his refusal to believe any longer in her phantasies, kills him. It is not too much to see in these two characters Fogazzaro's projection of his fears concerning the direction in which his youthful pursuit of the occult might have led him, and what might have happened to him—at least spiritually and psychologically—as a result, had he gone any farther.

A number of the lesser personages were drawn more or less directly from individuals whom Fogazzaro had known. The original of Steinegge was an Austrian ex-captain from whom the young Antonio had his first German lessons in Turin.[6] Césare d'Ormengo was, in real life, a friend of Mariano's in Milan—Abbondio Chialiva, an old revolutionary and former Carbonaro, liberal in politics and violently anticlerical.[7] Many of the others were also drawn from one or another of the guests and friends of the Fogazzaro family, from acquaintances of Mariano's or Antonio's in the political life of Vicenza, or from casual contacts made in Fogazzaro's travels.

The geographical background of *Malombra* is in part realistic, especially the scenes in Milan. On the other hand, the Count's palace is in an unidentifiable locality in the Brianza, the region north of Milan between the two arms of Lake Como, on an imaginary lake. (This lake is neither Lake Como nor Lake Lugano, since both are mentioned in the story.) Here too, however, Fogazzaro took certain specific features of localities known to him and transplanted them into the setting of the book, such as the *òrrido* into which Marina finally disappears. This is often identified with a cave on Lake Lugano. The Count's palace was drawn from one named the "Pliniana" on Lake Como.[8] In later novels, however, Fogazzaro almost always set the scene in houses, estates, and cities known to him. He would rename the real estate owned by individuals, but normally he kept the names of the cities. On occasion, he would make special visits to the latter in order to gather local color and exactitude in his references.

Fogazzaro's humor also makes its appearance for the first time, to any extent, in *Malombra*. The main characters are presented with great seriousness, especially Marina. Into the portrayal of many of the minor personages, however, there enters a large dose of humor, whether kind or unkind. With some characters, Fogazzaro makes us sympathize, but at the same time we smile at them, as at Steinegge in his idealistic but disillusioned liberalism. Steinegge introduces himself to Silla saying: "I hope that you will never write on your proscription-lists Andreas Gotthold Steinegge of Nassau, banished from his college for having loved wine too much, from his family for having loved women too much, from his country for having loved liberty too much. You know, my dear signor Silla, the last was the real folly."

Similarly, we sympathize with the servant-boy Rico in his adoration of Marina, which leads him to rejoice in a ridiculous livery in which to serve her.

Other characters, however, are clearly unsympathetic, and there is more than a touch of irony in the contrast between their pretensions and their pettiness of character. In *Malombra*, the chief such characters are the party of Venetian aristocrats—Marina's foppish suitor Nepo, his conceited mother Contessa Fosca, and the latter's garrulous servant Catte. Another favorite butt of Fogazzaro's ridicule is the type of narrow-minded, ultra-traditionalist, bigoted priest, which makes its first appearance in *Malombra* and recurs in many of his later stories. The humor of Fogazzaro's narration resides in the incongruity between what his characters do and the situation in which they find themselves, or between their words and what they are talking about. In *Malombra*, Fogazzaro uses little dialect, mostly Venetian and in the mouths of the Salvador group. Some of Fogazzaro's humorous portraits are so coherently effective as to have been called (favorably or unfavorably) *macchiette* "genre-portraits"; his humor goes, however, far beyond this relatively low level.

Yet with all the interest and suspense that the story arouses, the sympathy and the amusement that the reader feels, there remains something about Fogazzaro's *Malombra* which is, at first glance, difficult to explain. *Malombra* is certainly not, as some critics have suggested, simply a belated manifestation of the "Gothic" novel. Marina's insanity is clearly the central feature of the story, without which *Malombra* would simply be another tale of a man who could not decide between two women. It is not enough to call her madness unmotivated and arbitrary;[9] yet several questions remain. Why does Marina believe so firmly that she is the reincarnation of Cecilia? That she should bring about Count Ormengo's death is understandable in terms of the external plot; but why Silla? When she flees in the launch after shooting Silla, what actually happens to her? She disappears into the *òrrido*—but does she die there, or does she escape and live? (We are specifically told that there is a path leading away from the *òrrido* to an inn a kilometer away.) Might Fogazzaro not just as well have had Marina fail to kill Silla and drown in her attempted escape, so that he might marry Edith and live happily ever after? Most readers accept Marina's madness and the ending of the story as somehow "right"; but why? The answer lies in the further symbolism of the story and of its characters.

Corrado Silla is, as virtually all critics have recognized, the typical

Italian man of letters at an early stage of his development. He is not merely an autobiographical portrait. Some of his traits were never characteristic of Fogazzaro, even in his youth—for instance, his naïveté in personal relationships, and his inability to make up his mind, especially in matters of love and economics. Most of Fogazzaro's heroes learn and grow, intellectually and spiritually, in the course of the stories, but Silla does not. This is the cause of Silla's tragic end, because he has not understood the character of Marina nor the harm that she might do him.

Marina's self-identification with the past is what leads her to kill Césare d'Ormengo, and also—when he refuses to believe in it any longer—Silla as well. All of Fogazzaro's heroines can be interpreted as symbolizing one or another aspect of either Italian or foreign culture, depending on their origin. In this instance, Marina symbolizes that part of Italian culture which identifies itself with the past, and which believes that the Italian past has gone unrecognized and neglected or even maltreated by the modern world.[10] Cecilia Varrega, in this connection, stands for, not only one single figure out of the past, but all of earlier Italian culture. When the young writer falls in love with her and seems to share her belief in her identity with Cecilia, Marina is happy. When Silla no longer believes in this identity, even though he is still attracted to her as she is at present, she hates him and kills him as well as the Count who is the other chief representative of the modern world. Interpreted symbolically, this relationship and Marina's final act mean that the unrestrained adoration of the past is fatal for the modern Italian writer who cannot resist his initial infatuation. This danger was perhaps more real—given the persistence of old-fashioned classicism—in Fogazzaro's time than it is nowadays, but it has not yet wholly disappeared.

The uncertainty in which we are left concerning Marina's final disappearance is explained if we look at it in this light. She might conceivably escape (and Fogazzaro has one of the minor characters explicitly mention this possibility) or she might drown in the waters of the grotto. In all probability, Fogazzaro purposely left the upshot of her flight ambiguous. Perhaps Marina might survive, and return, in her present incarnation or in another form or under another name, to ruin the lives of other, equally credulous young writers. Similarly, a culture which has been falsely identified with the past might continue to infatuate and ruin Italian writers. The *òrrido* itself might be interpreted as the cave of fancy, where reality is so disfigured as to serve as a refuge for beautiful, attractive, but false ideas concerning the past, which do not die but only flee for a time when their falsity is demonstrated.

The secondary characters Césare d'Ormengo, Steinegge, and Edith are also significant from a cultural-symbolic point of view. The Count is the first of a series of older men, often eccentric but basically kindly, who appear in Fogazzaro's novels—Count Lao in *Daniele Cortis*, Uncle Piero in *Piccolo mondo antico*, the Marchese Scremin in *Piccolo mondo moderno*, and Marcello Trento in *Leila*. In *Malombra*, the Count has isolated himself from the modern world, living apart in a lonely palace, despising contemporary worldly society and remaining faithful to his conservative principles. Out of the kindness of his heart, however, he befriends Marina, saving her (as he thinks) from the superficiality and corruption of Parisian society, just as he later tries to rescue Silla from poverty and disorientation. The Count clearly represents that conservative segment of the Italian aristocracy who used to live (and some of whom still do live) isolated from the world, keeping alive a sub-culture which identifies itself with the past, but which kills (at least spiritually) those who keep it alive, as well as those who become infatuated with it.

The two Germans, Steinegge and Edith, form an essential part of the story since they are set off, both literally and symbolically, against Marina and, in a certain sense, also against Count d'Ormengo. One of the basic themes of Fogazzaro's work, as a whole, is the relation between Italian and European culture. In *Malombra*, the German refugee and his daughter clearly represent the latter. Silla falls in love with Edith, in the same way as an Italian man of letters might—and Fogazzaro did—become enamored of European, more specifically German culture. There inevitably arises a tension between Silla's love for Edith and his attraction to Marina.

The relation of Silla to Marina, on the one hand, and of Steinegge to Edith, on the other, furnishes an interesting contrast between Italian and German cultures. Marina, although she is physically young, considers herself the reïncarnation of Cecilia, and hence the relation between her and Silla is not only that between two lovers, but also that between two generations. Steinegge, on the other hand, is in fact Edith's father, and the relation between them is healthy and normal. Symbolically, the latter two represent the fundamentally healthy character of German culture, which—at least in those times—could survive separation due to historical accident, and in which there was lack of hostility, in fact there was love, between generations. In Italian culture, on the other hand, the almost magic attraction of the culture of the past is seen as harmful, and the past (symbolized by Marina-Cecilia) does not permit the modern Italian writer (Silla) to unite himself with foreign culture (Edith). On the contrary, it fascinates him only to destroy him.

Among the lesser characters, Don Innocenzo represents the good and healthy aspect of Christianity, which has more influence on non-Italians than on Italians. Edith and even her old, disillusioned father are more touched by Don Innocenzo's piety than is Silla. Rico, the boy-servant who naïvely adores Marina, is perhaps a symbol of the attitude of the common people towards Italian prestige-culture.

The symbolic message of *Malombra* is clear: the identification of Italian culture with the adoration of the past—which was (and still is) made by many, especially among the intelligentsia—is harmful, in fact fatal to modern Italian intellectual life. The name *Malombra*, too, is significant. One of Fogazzaro's ancestors came from a family named Malombra,[11] so that this feature of the novel, like so many others, had its origin in reality. Yet the symbolic interpretation of the name is quite obvious: the false identification of Italian culture with the past casts a *mala ombra*, an evil shade, over the present.

But how about foreign culture?—would it be possible for an Italian man of letters to "marry" himself to the culture of another land? The answer given in *Malombra* is negative. For Fogazzaro's further consideration of this problem, and his further answer, we must wait until Chapter 4, when we take up *Il mistero del poeta*.

CHAPTER 3

Love, Morality, and Politics

I An impossible love

THE year 1881 was a very important one in Fogazzaro's life.
His third and last child, Maria, was born on February 8.
Malombra was published after long delays in May, and was an immediate success. It earned high praise from many of Fogazzaro's
contemporaries, including his fellow-novelist Giovanni Verga,[1] and,
slightly later, the poet and dramatist Giuseppe Giacosa. At the end
of the same month, he began a new novel, *Daniele Cortis*,[2] which
was to occupy him for the next four years. He also wrote the first of
his many short stories, *Un pensiero di Ermes Torranza* ("A Thought
of Ermes Torranza"), which was published in the following year
(1882) as *Un'idea di Ermes Torranza*. At the beginning of
December, a twenty-five-year-old German girl, Felicitas Buchner,
from the Bavarian town of Eichstätt, came to live with the
Valmarana family as governess of Fogazzaro's nephew Angelo and
niece Ina.

Despite his patience and kindness, Fogazzaro's family-life in this
period was none too happy. He was devoted to his children Gina
and Mariano, to whose upbringing and intellectual development he
dedicated many hours. Rita, however, was becoming fussy and
shrewish, tending to treat her husband as if he were one of the
children, and showing little sympathy for his literary or aesthetic interests. His intellectual life was very active, with extensive reading
in German, French, and English; he even read the Finnish *Kalevala*
(in translation). His new novel was to deal with both politics and
religion; he therefore not only read widely in those fields, but made
his first trip to Rome, in the spring of 1882, to observe Parliament
and Roman life at first hand.

In this situation, it was in the cards that his affections might
wander in an extra-marital direction. Felicitas Buchner had been

35

taking Italian lessons from Giàcomo Zanella, reading the *Divine Comedy;* in 1882, she shifted to Fogazzaro with whom she worked (at first, not too successfully) on Manzoni's *Promessi sposi.* As the writing of *Daniele Cortis* progressed, Fogazzaro's interest in her became greater, despite the fact that she already had a fiancé in Germany. Some time in 1883, probably in the spring, their reciprocal affection grew stronger to the point of a mutual avowal in June. It was, however, an impossible situation, both legally and—from the point of view of Fogazzaro's strict conscience—morally.[3] On June 30, he made an entry in his diary (in English): *Friend, not lover. Never.* On July 3, he wrote: *Ho detto "no" all'amore / e leggo un libro santo* "I have said 'no' to love / and I read a holy book." Thenceforth, he cherished his love for Felicitas in his heart and, together with other poems, wrote one every July 3 to commemorate that date.[4] Outwardly, he remained on a level of friendship with her. She stayed in Italy, and Fogazzaro wrote to her frequently, often daily or even twice a day.[5] Felicitas broke off her engagement and spent the rest of her life in Italy, doing good works and never marrying. The historian wonders: did Fogazzaro fall in love with her for herself or did he rather project onto the unfortunate (and ironically misnamed) Felicitas his attachment to the type of heroine he had created in Miranda and in Edith—especially the latter, a pure German maiden?

II   Daniele Cortis

Fogazzaro's chief productions, in these years, were the two short stories *Un'idea di Ermes Torranza* and *Fedele,* the novel *Daniele Cortis,* and scattered lyrics. The novel was completed on March 11, 1884, and appeared in January of 1885, after some delay on the publisher's part. It was immediately successful, not so much because of the hero's political ideas (which Fogazzaro regarded as the most important feature of the story), as for the love-story and the romantic renunciation of the heroine.

The plot of *Daniele Cortis* is somewhat simpler than that of *Malombra.* The scene is laid, for the most part, at the Villa Carré, at Passo Rovese in the Venetian region. It belongs to Count Lao, the uncle of the heroine Èlena, who is married to a man much older than herself, the dissolute Sicilian wastrel Baron of Santa Giulia. To pay his debts, the Baron has Èlena ask for a loan from Count Lao, threatening to "exile" her to his estate at Cefalù in Sicily if he does not get the loan. Èlena goes to Cefalù, in part to get away from the proximity of her cousin Daniele Cortis. The latter lives near the Villa Carré and is a frequent visitor there; Èlena is beginning to feel an affection for Cortis which is too strong to be compatible with her duty to her husband—an affection which Daniele reciprocates.

Cortis is engaged in politics as a candidate for the House of Deputies. He advocates a strong monarchy, a serious social reform, and "a free church in a free state" as had been proposed by Cavour. Cortis wins the election (by one vote!) and goes to Rome to take his seat in Parliament. His affairs are complicated by the reappearance of his mother, an old harridan, who had abandoned him when he was small and had gone off with a lover. On Èlena's advice, he takes his mother in to live with him, but the situation becomes intolerable. Cortis arranges secretly for Èlena's husband's debts to be paid, only to find that it was the Baron of Santa Giulia for whom his mother had abandoned him. His psychological upset is so great that he goes to pieces just before making his maiden speech in Parliament. Considering himself a failure, he returns to Passo Rovese.

Èlena's husband has been told that if his debts are paid, he must leave Italy and go to America. Fearful that he may commit suicide, Èlena promises to accompany him. Before leaving, she goes to Villa Carré again, but finds Daniele's nearness disturbing. She wavers in her decision to accompany her husband. Both she and Daniele feel strong temptation, but overcome their mutual desire. At an evening musicale, Count Lao and his friend Senator Clenezzi sing an eighteenth-century aria[6] whose words sum up the situation between Daniele and Èlena. She and he "sit it out", but she refuses to tell him why she will not play or sing; she has already made up her mind to go. The next day, they decide not to ever see or write to each other again. Their only hope is for a reunion of their spirits in the beyond, through mystic communion in God. The Baron learns that he is to go to Yokohama rather than America; Èlena departs for Venice to embark with him there. Cortis feels that he has been strengthened by the trials through which he has passed and by his renunciation. He prepares to reënter political life and fight anew for his ideals.

The action of *Daniele Cortis* takes place over a relatively short period of time, from June 28, 1881, to April 18, 1882. In June of 1881, Italy had been united for less than eleven years[7] as a constitutional monarchy under the House of Savoy. For the first six years, Parliament was controlled by a conservative majority, the

Grande Destra or "Great Right." The *Destra* laid its prime emphasis on sound finances—essential in a country as weak, poor, and in need of major improvements as Italy was—and reconciliation, as far as possible, with the Vatican. In 1876, the *Destra* was replaced by the *Sinistra* or "Left," whose opposition to the Right consisted mainly of anticlericalism and demands for wider popular suffrage, tougher diplomacy in foreign affairs, and a stronger military machine. Both parties were, in practice, equally devoted to civil liberties, which both wished to preserve and extend as far as possible—a difficult job in the atmosphere of extremism and violence which was rampant at the time. In 1882, the electorate was expanded by the inclusion of large numbers of voters from the lower classes. The necessity for creating, under these circumstances, a more durable government, drawing on all factions, was met by a system of mutual accommodation and shifting of ground as was rendered necessary by events, not unlike the American two-party system. This basically healthy *de facto* coalition of the two parties was known by the opprobrious epithet of *trasformismo* ("transformism"), applied to it by ideologues who wished to see no compromise made, even if it were necessary in order to assure the stability of the government and the country.[8]

The situation was complicated by the hostility of Pope Pius IX and his successor Leo XIII to the new state of affairs. In the first part of the nineteenth century, a movement known as Neo-Guelfism[9] had favored the unification of Italy under papal rule. Exactly the opposite had taken place in 1870. When Rome was taken, all vestiges of papal temporal power disappeared. There were those who considered this development to be a blessing in disguise for Catholicism, since the pope could now devote all his energies to spiritual matters.[10] Pius IX, however, did not see the situation in this light. He virtually immured himself within the walls of the Vatican, refusing even to recognize the legitimacy of the constitutional monarchy or to receive any overtures aimed at reconciliation with it. He issued, and Leo XIII reconfirmed—later modifying it slightly— a decree known as the *non expedit* "it is not fitting," i.e., for devout Catholics to take any part in Italian politics or to vote in elections. This attitude of uncompromising hostility was spread by the more conservative members of the clergy and their lay followers. Clerical influence in this respect was especially strong in the Vèneto. Vicenza was a stronghold of ultrareactionary clericalism, which Fogazzaro had the opportunity of observing in all its details in the local clergy and laymen.

Many romantic idealists, especially among men of letters, regretted the passing of what they considered the noble, heroic days of the Risorgimento, and their replacement by a prosaic, bureaucratic government whose only concern was with budgets and administration. This feeling was expressed in violent terms by the anticlerical, classicist poet Giosuè Carducci (1835 - 1904), who lost no opportunity of comparing the supposedly pedestrian, bourgeois parliamentarianism of the post-Risorgimento with the glories of ancient Rome. Carducci's popularity as a poet aided in the dissemination of his antiparliamentarian views, especially among young and restless students. The hypercritical intelligentsia, with strong emotions, unrealistic fancies, and great verbal skill, but with little understanding of economic and military realities, kept girding at what they considered the unheroic, corrupt institutions of parliamentary government. Unfortunately, as Thayer has observed, "from Lamartine to d'Annunzio the literati have taken delight in stirring up trouble with which statesmen must deal as best they may, armed with the weapons of politics, which often have little effect against the rhetoric of poets. [. . .] Frequently political reformers who believed in democracy unwittingly served its enemies, and their own, by joining the chorus of derision."[11]

The nascent parliamentary democracy of Italy was further beset by the immense problems caused by the reunion of the northern and the southern parts of the peninsula, which had been separated for almost fifteen hundred years. Due to a complex of historical factors, the Mezzogiorno, or southern Italy, was far behind the north in its economic and intellectual development. Its assimilation into the new united Italy was rendered very difficult by widespread poverty and illiteracy.[12] The introduction of universal military service and greatly increased taxation, in part necessary to support a continually growing bureaucracy modelled on that of Piedmont, created great resentment—and, in some instances, outright revolt—in the Mezzogiorno. The taxes were necessary to pay for the modernization of the country, and the bureaucracy was, at least in part, necessary to administer it; but that did not lessen the unpopularity of the new order in the Mezzogiorno. Northern Italians, on the other hand, often regarded the South as virtually a foreign country, its citizens as backward and its annexation as a drag on the new nation.[13]

In the midst of this struggle between so many diverse and hostile factions, one relatively small group, while deploring the "mess" in Rome, wished to see democratic government preserved, but with Christian principles brought into a completely lay, non-confessional state. They hoped for the abolition of the papal *non expedit*, so that moderate Catholics might, with a clear conscience, take part in the political life of Italy. These hopes were still realistic in the early 1880's. It was not until 1887 that Padre Tosti's celebrated pamphlet *Conciliazione*, urging the abandonment of the Papal claims to temporal power for the sake of a united Italy, was slapped down by the Vatican at the instigation of ultraconservative forces, and the hopes of liberal Catholics were dashed.[14] Yet, in historical perspective, it is clear that the liberal Catholics, although their views were rejected by both sides, were the force that kept the new Italian nation from splitting into two completely irreconcilable groups, clerical and anticlerical.[15]

This excursus on the political and religious situation in Italy in the 1870's and 1880's has been necessary as a background for the understanding of *Daniele Cortis*. In the novel, Fogazzaro achieves a remarkable fusion of the several aspects of the contemporary scene—political, ethical, moral, religious—as they affected both private and public life. Cortis himself obviously reflects Fogazzaro's own views, so far as these matters are concerned. In a letter written in 1908,[16] Fogazzaro said:

the political ideas of my protagonist—who, incidentally, professed and practised traditional Catholicism; he was in no wise a religious reformer—can be briefly summarized as follows: a strong monarchy, able to take high-level political action, without the guide and tutelage of parliamentary majorities, and capable of taking bold initiatives in the field of social reform; a state freed from any ties to any church, but convinced that social problems cannot be solved successfully without the coöperation of religious feeling, which can be furnished in Italy only by the Catholic Church; respectful, and not hostile, application of the general law to this Church, and therefore recognition of religious associations which do not have an illegal aim; abolition of religious teaching given by the civilian authorities, and the obligation to have it from the clergy.

Daniele's ideal was essentially what he was apparently the first to term *democrazia cristiana* "Christian democracy". Later critics[17] have unjustly blamed Fogazzaro for what they considered the misdeeds of the strongly clerical *Democrazia Cristiana* party of the post-Second-World-War years.

Fogazzaro had a great admiration for Count Bismarck, and drew some of the features of Daniele Cortis from him. His admiration has seemed strange to later generations, who remember Bismarck only as the "Iron Chancellor" and the duplicitous diplomat of the Ems telegram. Fogazzaro, however, believed that he could perceive a certain "childlike kindness" hidden inside the Chancellor's iron character.[18] What he admired in Bismarck's political activity was the latter's firmness and strength in carrying out his policies. Daniele's (and hence Fogazzaro's) call for a strong executive has been interpreted as an anticipation of Fascism, as when Luigi Russo said: "But this, alas, is basically the program that was realized in Fascism, and we know who was the Italian Bismarck. Thus, according to Fogazzaro's views, the Democrazia Cristiana and Fascism were born at the same time."[19] In fact, however, Fogazzaro was simply wishing for a relationship between king and parliament similar to that of Franklin D. Roosevelt, Truman, or Kennedy to the American Congress (not, we hasten to add, that of a Nixon!).[20] Mussolini was no Bismarck, and Fogazzaro was in no wise a proto-Fascist.

Daniele is not, however, simply a projection of Fogazzaro's own personality onto an imaginary political campaign and parliamentary activity. Fogazzaro made of Daniele a considerably more practical man than he himself was, and more oriented towards immediate action with respect to the problems of the moment. Daniele is also much less aesthetically and musically inclined than Fogazzaro himself was. Much has been made of supposed "weaknesses" of Daniele's character, both in failing to take advantage of Èlena's love for him by seducing her, and in being so emotionally moved as to collapse just before giving his maiden speech in the Chamber of Deputies.[21] The former criticism is of course based on the vulgar conception of the "Latin" male as sexually strong, and hence contemptible if he does not take every opportunity to prove his masculinity—an attitude known in Italy as *gallismo*, "rooster-like behavior," and in Spain and Latin America as *machismo*. The Piccionis report[22] a conversation at Fogazzaro's table in which a guest said of Daniele, in Milanese dialect, *L'è on omm che l'è minga on omm* "He's a man who's not at all a man." Daniele's collapse will be discussed later, in connection with the cultural symbolism of his character.

Èlena, on the other hand, was immediately popular and pleased virtually all readers, especially for what normal people considered the lofty morality of her and Daniele's renunciation of their mutual love. Even one of Fogazzaro's strongest critics[23] called Èlena "the figure from whom a whole generation learned an ideal." She states specifically that she takes marriage too seriously to contemplate adultery, and is therefore ready to follow her unworthy husband into exile. In writing *Cortis*, Fogazzaro was uncertain as to whether he should give the story a "happy" ending, perhaps having the Baron of Santa Giulia vanish or commit suicide.[24] Both Fogazzaro's personal experience with Felicitas, however, and his (perhaps unconscious) insight into the cultural situation persuaded him to adopt what most readers feel instinctively is the "right" solution. He also thought of Èlena's and Daniele's desire to be united only spiritually in the hereafter as a manifestation of the evolution of humanity from a lower to a higher sphere, of the type he advocated in his essays[25] as reconciling the doctrine of evolution with Christianity.

Even at the time *Daniele Cortis* was published, however, and later, some critics objected to the love of Daniele and Èlena as involving a "spiritual adultery," in no wise moral, in fact more immoral than outright physical adultery because they considered "spiritual adultery" hypocritical. Like Benedetto Croce,[26] some considered Fogazzaro's morality as "erotic" because he described Daniele's and Èlena's temptations in detail and with sympathy. (But how else is the novelist to persuade the reader of the reality and intensity of their temptation, and of the effort required to overcome it?) The concept of "spiritual adultery" is virtually a contradiction in terms, and rests on the assumption—characteristic of the less enlightened areas of Mediterranean culture—that a woman's spirit, as well as her body, is forever her husband's property, both in life and after death. Such a concept is directly in contradiction with the Christian doctrine that in heaven there is neither marriage nor giving in marriage.[27] Both Daniele and Èlena grow spiritually through their sufferings and sacrifices, and acquire psychological strength to face the tasks that lie ahead of them—Daniele in his return to political life, Èlena in her self-imposed exile with her husband in Yokohama. Not for nothing did Fogazzaro give his hero the name of Daniele, recalling the Biblical story of him who passed through the lions' den.

True to his custom, Fogazzaro drew many of the personages of *Daniele Cortis* from living persons. Èlena was originally a portrait of

Fogazzaro's cousin by marriage, the Marchesa Angelica Mangilli Lampertico, who had the same appearance and characteristics as Èlena—slender, tall, with large eyes and a lively intelligence, fond of books and flowers. Later, after his experience with Felicitas Buchner, Fogazzaro infused into Èlena's psychology a great deal of Felicitas' spiritual conflict and final acceptance of the impossibility of her love. Felicitas was not unlike the Marchesa in her appearance as well, as can be seen by comparing the portraits of the two.[28] Among the lesser characters, Count Lao reflects Fogazzaro's father-in-law, Count Angelo di Valmarana. For the narrow-minded, bigoted clerical reactionaries, of whom there are a number in the novel, Fogazzaro had plenty of models in Vicenza.

The scenes in which *Daniele Cortis* is laid are also based on reality. Villa Carré is a direct portrayal of the Villa Valmarana, and Passo di Rovese is Velo d'Àstico. Èlena's reading-room and her desk are Fogazzaro's own. The brooks and trees are those of the surrounding country-side. Even the dead cypress covered with wisteria, which we already met in *Miranda*, was real, standing between two of the buildings at Villa Valmarana.[29] The city is clearly Vicenza, and Rome, too, is described in great detail with the action set in real localities, such as the Chamber of Deputies at Montecitorio and the Hotel Minerva in the centre of the city.

Fogazzaro's humor is even more important in *Daniele Cortis* than in *Malombra*. It is present in the genre-portraits of unsympathetic characters, such as the narrow-minded priests and their reactionary lay supporters, and the Baron of Santa Giulia, in whose mouth Fogazzaro puts several characteristic Sicilianisms. It also serves, on occasion, to relax the emotional tension after a crisis. Thus, after Èlena and Daniele have sat through the music-making at Villa Carré, and the party is over: "In the drawing-room there was no longer any-one. Lao, Clenezzi, and Countess Tarquinia had returned to the piano-room, where the first-mentioned was playing the aria from *L'Olimpiade* with youthful enthusiasm, and Clenezzi was wretchedly sobbing out its words."

Who is the central character in *Daniele Cortis?* Despite the name of the novel, many readers and critics have regarded Èlena as a more impressive and memorable, and hence more central figure than Daniele. Such a view, however, is based on a narrowly aesthetic and romantic approach, regarding the emotional and "poetic" side of the story as its only important characteristic, and denying the literary relevance or value of all its other facets. If we take into account the total message of the book—not merely its personal, emotional aspects, but its cultural and more specifically political content as well—we see that the book's title is correct. Daniele symbolizes the moral and political responsibilities which were (and still are) incumbent on post-1870 Italy. He represents the modern Italian, not in artistic or aesthetic matters, but in his practical and political aspects.[30] Modern Italian society has had to be reborn, overcoming the difficulties that it has inherited from its political and social past. But the modern Italian, in Fogazzaro's view, has to go through immense travail on this account, over almost unsurmountable obstacles, and sacrificing even what is most dear to him.[31]

In order to achieve this goal, Fogazzaro suggests, the first thing that the modern Italian must learn is the necessity for a solid, firm, and straightforward conscience, directed, not by rules imposed from outside, but by the principles of Christian morality which he has internalized and made his own. He must be, to use David Riesman's term,[32] inner-directed. The attainment of this goal will be difficult, and, at the outset, a man with ideals of this type, even if he persuades a large enough number of his fellow-citizens, will do so by a very small majority. Cortis is elected deputy by a majority of only one.

The new "homo politicus", whom Daniele represents, will have difficulties because of the present situation and also because of the past, whose errors and sins will keep turning up to block his way. Daniele's mother symbolizes the past. A figure of ill omen but necessary for the development of the story, she symbolizes the unsavory and shady origin of much of Italian political life. The difficulties which this family drama causes Daniele are the reason for his stroke and collapse in Parliament. In exactly the same way, the "homo politicus" of modern Italy has had to suffer doubts and anguish, such as the troubles caused, not long after *Daniele Cortis* was written, by enemies of democracy such as Carducci, Oriani,[33] and other precursors of fascism. The result of these troubles was the collapse of Italian democracy during and after the First World War. Without Cortis' mother, without the difficulties that she causes her son in the story and doubtless might be expected to keep on causing him later—note that she remains alive and is presumably still alive at the end of the novel—the drama of *Daniele Cortis* would be shorn of one of its essential features. After the crisis in his family and his love, however, Cortis recovers his strength and is able to return with new vigor to political life.

Èlena symbolizes the culture and the society of northern Italy, especially in their most lofty manifestations. Èlena is married to a Sicilian, and this fact, too, is symbolically important. The Baron of Santa Giulia stands for those unpleasant aspects of Italian, particularly South Italian, life to which Italian society is indissolubly wedded. He represents the dissoluteness, the corruption, and the brutality about which northern Italians have always complained. In short, the "homo politicus" of modern Italy cannot have northern Italy for himself, because it is already—in the view of northern Italians—chained to southern Italy, with which it will have to keep on living forever, despite the latter's undesirable characteristics. The exile of Èlena and her husband symbolizes the forced separation of Italian society from its ideals, with which it can be reunited only at some future time—which Fogazzaro recognized might be long in coming, but for which he nevertheless hoped.

Fogazzaro's message in *Daniele Cortis* is, briefly, this: that the "homo politicus" of modern Italy will have to carry out his plans in the world as it is, recognizing above all the indissoluble union of the entire peninsula, and overcoming the insufficiencies of Italian life which the country has inherited from centuries of misrule. He will also have to raise himself (and, thereby, his country) to a higher moral level through renunciation and sacrifice, purifying himself and battling for a government which is honest, firm, and devoted to the well-being of the country. In *Daniele Cortis*, Fogazzaro was (as he himself recognized) advocating a generalized, over-all program, not making detailed proposals with regard to specific issues. This approach was, however, the best one to take with regard to the long-range solution of the country's moral and ethical problems as a whole, rather than getting mired down in the morass of short-term, shifting issues.

For a time after Fogazzaro's death in 1911, *Daniele Cortis* was widely considered to be his second best novel, next to *Piccolo Mondo Antico*. After the Second World War, opinion changed—especially under the influence of Marxist doctrines, according to which Fogazzaro was to blame for advocating a type of political morality at variance with Marxist orthodoxy—so that many critics preferred *Malombra* to *Cortis*. A more balanced approach, however, leads us to the recognition that Fogazzaro succeeded very well in fusing the treatment of political problems with those of personal emotions, on their common basis of ethics and morality. *Daniele Cortis* remains very readable, holds the reader's interest at a high point throughout, and at the same time leads the unprejudiced observer to understanding and sympathy for its hero's dilemma with regard to both Èlena and his country.

CHAPTER 4

The Poet and Foreign Culture

I Success at Last

FOGAZZARO was almost forty-three when *Daniele Cortis* appeared. *Miranda* and *Valsolda* had gone almost unnoticed by the general public; *Malombra* had enjoyed a certain amount of popularity. *Cortis*, however, was widely read and aroused a great deal of discussion. Fogazzaro was now famous. From this time on, he was a popular author and publishers vied for his works. In addition to his novels and poems, he wrote a number of *novelle*, which began to appear in this period and which were later collected in several volumes. The first of these short stories, *Un'idea di Ermes Torranza* (1881), still reflects some of Fogazzaro's interest in occultism. It is the story of a young couple, Bianca and Emilio, who have separated. Knowing that they still love each other, Ermes Torranza—an old poet who is a friend of theirs—concocts a plan to bring them together again. He arranges that, after his death, Bianca is to be at a certain time in the music-room of her house, and is to play Weber's *Dernière pensée musicale* ("Last Musical Thought"). Emilio has been told to stand outside the house and, if she plays this, to take it as a sign that she still loves him. It goes as Torranza has planned, and the two are reconciled as if by some mystic force. *Ermes Torranza* is, for the balance of the psychic and the every-day aspects of the tale, and for Fogazzaro's skill in creating a "misty" atmosphere, perhaps his best short story. It may also have symbolized his desire to be, in some way, even after his death, one of the forces that would reunite the conflicting factions in Italy.

The best of the other short stories which he wrote in these years are *Eden Anto, Fedele*, and *Il fiasco del Maestro Chieco* (all published in 1885). *Eden Anto* is perhaps Fogazzaro's most intense portrayal of complete disappointment and disillusionment. Vasco, a bankrupt old lawyer, is being pressed by his crassly greedy creditor

47

Marcòn for payment of a debt. The only things of value that Vasco has left is a sixteenth-century edition of Ariosto with the cryptic words EDEN ANTO over the design on the front page. Vasco is proud of his interpretation of these words as equivalent to the Greek for "it burned flowering." He has planned to leave the Ariosto as a legacy to the town library. Marcòn tries to take the volume in payment for the debt, but Vasco, rather than have it pass into unworthy hands, places it on the fire, where it "burns flowering." After Marcòn has left in a rage, a young priest comes to tell Vasco that his interpretation of the two words was wrong. They should be read F. DE NANTO, the name of the sixteenth-century engraver who cut the design. Vasco's hopes and his only valued possession have been destroyed, and his illusions concerning the meaning of EDEN ANTO have been shattered. He dies the same night.

In *Eden Anto*, somewhat atypically, there is no mention of music. In the other two *novelle*, music plays a central part. In *Fedele*, a woman named Fedele ("faithful") has, many years previously, angered her father by marrying against his wishes. He is now blind, and she implores his forgiveness by singing the aria "Pietà, Signore" ("Have mercy, Lord", formerly ascribed to the composer Alessandro Stradella), but he is unmoved. *Il fiasco del Maestro Chieco*, on the contrary, is a humorous story, in which the narrator tells of the failure of the plans of his friend, the eccentric 'cellist Chieco (modelled after Fogazzaro's Milanese acquaintance Gaetano Braga). Chieco is enamored of a certain lady, and arranges a party for her. At the gathering, it turns out that the lady is a former flame of the narrator. Chieco's plans gang agley, in that the meeting leads to the reconciliation of the narrator and his lady-love. As might be expected, *Maestro Chieco* is told with a great deal of vigor and humor. There are also humorous touches in *Ermes Torranza* and *Eden Anto* (for instance, in the comparison of the heavy-set Vasco and Marcòn to two hippopotami), but none in *Fedele*.

In addition to these *novelle*, Fogazzaro also wrote a certain number of lyrics, some of which were included in his stories, a few were published separately, and many—intended for his *Libro dell'amore immortale*—remained unpublished. In August of 1884, his belovèd maternal uncle, Pietro Barrera, died. Fogazzaro remembered gratefully how Pietro had generously sacrificed his share of the family inhertance to enable his sister Teresa and Mariano Fogazzaro to marry.[1] Antonio decided to write a story which should include a character based on his uncle Pietro, who would be a beneficient angel for a young couple in the same way. This was the genesis of the novel which Fogazzaro originally intended to call *Storia quieta*, "Quiet Story" (in contrast to the drama of *Malombra* and *Daniele Cortis*), and which eventually grew into *Piccolo mondo antico*. He jotted down a preliminary outline of the story and the names of the characters on August 16, 1884.[2]

II Il mistero del poeta

In 1883, while staying at Oria, Fogazzaro had spent some time at an out-of-the-way hotel, the Belvedere, on top of the mountain in back of Lanzo d'Intelvi, which is across Lake Lugano from the Valsolda. Here he met a young American lady, Miss Ellen Starbuck—blonde, blue-eyed, short-sighted, with a slight limp and a dulcet voice, delicate in health and with a veiled sorrow in her glance. Fogazzaro struck up a friendship with Ellen Starbuck, which over the years gave rise to an increasingly close but non-amorous epistolary friendship. His letters to her are as valuable a source of information for his later years as are those to Felicitas for his middle life. As was his custom with various feminine acquaintances and correspondents, he tried to convert her, in this case from Protestantism to Catholicism, but without success.

Up to this time, Fogazzaro had travelled extensively in northern Italy and Italian Switzerland, and had made one trip to Rome to gather material for *Daniele Cortis*. Outside of Italy, he made only a one-day trip to Nice, in January of 1884.[3] He had hopes of visiting Germany in the same year,[4] but was not able to do so until May, 1885. Felicitas' sisters Eleonore and Toni welcomed him in Munich, showing him the sights there and then taking him to Eichstätt, where the Buchner family had previously lived. The rest of Fogazzaro's itinerary took him to Nürnberg, Heidelberg, Frankfurt am Main, the Rhineland and the Black Forest.

After beginning the first draft of *Storia quieta*, Fogazzaro laid it aside for other matters. A satirical short story, *Pereat Rochus* ("Let Rocco perish"), dealing with an idealistic but naïve and gullible priest, Don Rocco, appeared in January, 1886. Beginning in that year, Fogazzaro held various minor political positions in Vicenza—an experience which he undoubtedly used later in his portrayal of municipal administration in *Piccolo mondo moderno*. He suffered a major emotional blow in the death of his father Mariano on April 11, 1887. He was still tormented by his love for Felicitas, recording his struggles against temptation in a private diary. The writing of his next novel, *Il mistero del poeta* ("The Mystery of the Poet") undoubtedly served to sublimate this emotion, and he was able to finish it in what for him was record time—from November, 1884, to mid-1887. It appeared the next year, first in serial form and then as a book.

Il mistero del poeta is told in the first person by an unnamed narrator, nine years after the events recounted. He meets, at the Hotel Belvedere at Lanzo d'Intelvi, a delicate young woman, blonde, blue-eyed, short-sighted, with a slight limp and a dulcet voice, delicate in health and with a veiled sorrow in her glance. The narrator immediately falls in love with her. He discovers that her name is Violet Yves; she is half English and half Italian, but has been brought up in Germany, as a Catholic, by relatives in the small Bavarian city of Eichstätt. The narrator declares his love, but she says that she is already engaged to a school-teacher in Eichstätt. She cannot break this engagement because of a former entanglement which, she hints darkly, involved something dishonorable. Violet begs the narrator not to seek any further contact with her. He is so enamored of her, however, that he disobeys and follows her after she has left Lanzo d'Intelvi. He traces her to Naples, Rome, and thence to Germany, where the central section of the story takes place.

The narrator catches up with Violet—to her displeasure—at Nürnberg. By chance, he makes the acquaintance of her fiancé's elder brother Stephan Topler,[3] to whom he often refers humorously as *Toplerus senior*. Similarly, the younger brother, Hans, is frequently called *Toplerus junior*. Together with Violet and her friend Luise von Dobra, the narrator and Toplerus senior take the train for Eichstätt. After their arrival, the group have an idyllic picnic in the woods between the station and the town, and the narrator has a number of pleasant social contacts during his stay in Eichstätt. He becomes very friendly with Toplerus senior, on the basis of a mutual interest in music, while at the same time he is inundating Violet with letters and poems to persuade her of his unshakable love. Her engagement to Hans, who is also sickly, has been undertaken on the understanding that they were to have a *mariage blanc*. Violet admits that she has felt attracted to the young Italian, but her puritanical conscience has prevented her from returning his love. She finally consents to marry him. Toplerus junior agrees, despite his bitter disappointment, to give Violet her freedom so that she can marry her Italian suitor. The latter is warned by the Topler brothers that Violet's health is precarious; any excitement might prove fatal to her. Violet is afraid that the man with whom she was entangled in the past might return to cause difficulties, so it is decided that the wedding shall take place somewhere else. After a short visit to his home in Italy, the narrator returns to Germany, meeting Violet at the estate of some English friends at Rüdesheim, on the Rhine. They take several excursions, on one of which they unexpectedly meet Violet's former lover. The latter has searched everywhere for her, and threatens to kill himself if he cannot have her. Violet and the narrator are finally married at Rüdesheim. They take the train for Wiesbaden, but her former lover is also on the train. Despite the narrator's warnings, the former lover presents himself at the window of the compartment. His appearance gives Violet such a shock that she dies of heart-failure. The narrator is inconsolable, but he continues to adore her memory and feels that she is eternally with him in spirit.

So far as her appearance and physical characteristics are concerned, Violet Yves is clearly drawn from Ellen Starbuck. For a long time, it was thought that Miss Starbuck had been the object of Fogazzaro's unnamed love, and (perhaps also because of the similarity of the name) the original of Èlena in *Daniele Cortis*. In Eichstätt, however, it was realized quite early on that Violet's real prototype was Felicitas Buchner. Luise von Dobra, likewise, was drawn from Felicitas' sister Eleonore. Felicitas' fiancé was named Tobler, but the elder brother is a creation of Fogazzaro's imagination. The other minor personages whom the narrator meets in Eichstätt are also reflections of people whom Fogazzaro knew there at the time of his visit. Fogazzaro's interest in Eichstätt is still remembered there.[4]

By this time, Fogazzaro had acquired the habit of using only really existing places for the scenes of his novels. All of the settings of *Il mistero del poeta* are named by their actual names, and described in extensive detail: Lanzo d'Intelvi, the Hotel Belvedere, Munich, Nürnberg, Eichstätt, and a number of lesser places along the Rhine between Mainz and Köln. Even the hotel in Eichstätt where the narrator stays, and the streets of the town are given their real names as of the time of the story. For many years, Fogazzaro had been in the habit of writing to his family, and later to Felicitas, giving detailed descriptions of the places he visited in his travels. The unnamed narrator of the *Mistero* gives similarly detailed relations, skillfully dovetailing his accounts of the localities together with the story of his and Violet's emotional experiences. The descriptions are so accurate as to enable a modern visitor to Eichstätt to recognize streets and houses even when their present names are no longer those of Fogazzaro's day.[5]

Il mistero del poeta, despite the detailed realism of Fogazzaro's description of the external settings, is the only one of his novels to be entirely free of concern with political or social matters.[6] Its only overt theme is the love of the narrator and Violet for each other, its gradual development and sudden destruction through her death just at the point of expected fulfillment. In this respect, it is comparable to Dante's *Vita nuova*, which has aptly been called "the autobiography of an emotion." Another major resemblance of the *Mistero* to the *Vita nuova* is the large part which lyric poetry plays in each. Fogazzaro worked into the *Mistero* a number of the poems which he had written for Felicitas. They are an integral part of the developing story, carefully woven into its fabric so that each poem comes naturally at the point where it is introduced. On the other hand, Fogazzaro eschews the somewhat dry, scholastic analyses which Dante gives for each of his poems.

Music plays an important part in *Il mistero del poeta*, but only in the Eichstätt episode. The narrator and his friends sing German folk-songs—dealing, of course, with love—at the picnic. There are *Lieder* and other kinds of music at the home of the Treubergs, where Violet is staying, and at the von Dobras'. His initial friendship with Toplerus senior is on the basis of the latter's playing him a composition which he at first passes off as early Italian:

I shall never be able to forget the figure of the bent-over little old man moving his long nose to the right and to the left above the key-board, following the even and agile movement of his hands. Those lean fingers, clinging to the keys like hooks, sounded out, although they almost seemed not to be moving, a quiet, very smooth, serene music with a few hints of affection and humor.

From time to time I exclaimed "Beautiful!", and he would laugh quietly, while playing; then he said, continuing to play, "Do you know who it is by? Do you know who it is by?". I named a few of our old masters. He laughed, played, and did not answer.

"Toplerus," he said to me when he had finished the piece. "Toplerus senior, village organist."

I believe that I wholly won his heart that evening.

Whereas the passage just quoted involves music-making and listening by the main personages and serves to characterize them, it serves in other episodes as a background, setting the emotional tone for the narrator's reaction, as in the scene where he listens, in the public square, to German poetry and song coming from within his friends' house:

As I came into the Rossmarkt, I heard playing and singing. The windows of the Treubergs' house were open and the sound was coming directly from there. [. . .] A baritone sang detestably something by Wagner,[7] and then a fresh young woman's voice sang gracefully Schubert's *Haidenröslein*, which I had already heard being sung on a mild November afternoon, in the midst of the last roses of my Italian hillside. At that time Goethe's simple poem and Schubert's simple music, with that carefree gaiety of theirs full of hidden melancholy, had clutched at my heart; now they caused me a spasm of jealous pain, now I wrung my hands because the sweet *Röslein auf der Haide*, the little rose on the heath, was merged in my innermost mind with my little rose, with the little rose of the bitter tale. [. . .] I could stand it no longer and I came away.

In *Il mistero del poeta*, the narrator-poet undoubtedly reflects, in very large part, Fogazzaro's own attitude towards Italian and foreign cultures. We know, from many direct and indirect sources, that his cultural interests were extensive, ranging from Chateaubriand and Victor Hugo to Heine, Shakespeare, and the Finnish *Kalevala*. In this regard, he was similar to Longfellow, who made translations from many languages and modelled his *Hiawatha* (1856) on the *Kalevala*. Fogazzaro was of course not hostile to Italian literature and music. In the latter field, his preferences were definitely for what he termed *musica italiana antica* "old Italian music." By this, he meant "of the eighteenth and early nineteenth centuries"—Corelli, Tartini, Pergolesi, and so forth, down to Bellini—and his likings reflected his own personal contacts with literature and music. For the music and the literature of his own time, Fogazzaro had much less sympathy. This we know from many observations scattered throughout his correspondence and his stories, both expressions of specific dislike for contemporary authors and composers, and *obiter dicta* like this one from *Un'idea di Ermes Torranza:* "[. . .] *Rob Roy, Waverly,* and *Ivanhoe,* three poor old books of the family's scanty library, three poor old immortal books which are now waiting on their shelf for other eager hands, other ardent hearts unfamiliar with our great modern art."

Fogazzaro's preoccupation with foreign, particularly Nordic, culture is easily recognizable, and justifies our identification of Violet Yves with that culture. We note that Violet is half Italian and half English, just as English culture itself was, under Italian influence, from Chaucer to Milton, and as French and German culture also were from the Renaissance onwards, up to authors such as Stendhal and Goethe. Although her father was Protestant, Violet was brought up as a Catholic, thus showing Fogazzaro's preference for those aspects of North European religious life that were closest to his own beliefs. Violet is by no means, as she has been called,[8] the symbol of "an unmotivated flight from reality"; she is the symbol of all non-Italian European culture. The union of the poet-narrator with Violet clearly symbolizes Fogazzaro's hope that Italian culture might be reunited with those aspects of north European life which are related to it and in which the Italian man of letters might find a new inspiration. The narrator's hopes for a happy life with Violet reflect Fogazzaro's hopes for an equally happy and fruitful "marriage" between the two cultures, Italian and north European, as exemplied in his own work and foreseen by him in "the great poet of the future."[9]

But Violet is not to be his. The narrator-poet succeeds in winning her from her fiancé, Toplerus junior, who is a sickly, humble, honest, and colorless little school-teacher. Violet's projected marriage with him would have been quiet and without sexual intercourse, hence sterile. Another important point is that Toplerus junior is a Lutheran. Protestant readers of *Il mistero del poeta* do not greatly like this aspect of the story, and find it at first difficult to sympathize with this Catholic narrator who robs the unfortunate Lutheran professor of his fiancée, only to bring her to a death which deprives them both of the beloved. Here, particularly, we must keep in mind the symbolic value of the relationship between the three. Toplerus junior represents the modern life of small German towns, which, according to the symbolism of the story, is unfavorable and harmful to the culture of those places. Violet is sickly as a result of her stay in Germany, and is better only in Italy. North European culture would develop much more happily in union with Italian intellectual life. This symbolism is the justification for the narrator's action, which appears on the surface to be selfish and cruel.

What about the "other man" in Violet's life? She speaks of him on occasion in veiled fashion as of a previous lover, in a shameful episode that she does not wish to remember or discuss. At the end of the novel, when he appears at the window of the compartment, Violet dies of shock. Here, too, the outcome may seem somewhat unmotivated, except in the light of its symbolism. Violet's mysterious lover represents those elements, in the Italian origins of North European culture, which are shameful and dishonorable. We may cite, for instance, the reputation of Machiavelli during the entire sixteenth, seventeenth, and eighteenth centuries up to the *Anti-Machiavel* (1740) of that most Machiavellian king, Frederick II of Prussia. We may also remember the English view of the morals of Italians, as summed up in the sixteenth-century proverb current in England, *Inglese italianato, uomo indiavolato* "An Italianate Englishman is a man possessed by the Devil". English dramatists often presented Italians as amoral, scheming, and villainous, from Ben Jonson's *Volpone* (1606) to Percy Bysshe Shelley's *The Cenci* (1819). Here we are dealing, of course, not with the Italians as they actually were, but with the idea which Europeans had formed, rightly or wrongly, of Italian culture during the Renaissance and the immediately following period.

Violet dies on seeing this man reappear out of her past; similarly, the cultural hopes of the Italian poet for a reunion with North European culture are dashed by the unfavorable concept which the bearers of the latter have concerning Italy, due to the latter country's presumably shameful past. For the modern Italian man of letters there remains, therefore, only the possibility of concerning himself with modern, nineteenth-century Italy; and this was, in fact, Fogazzaro's concern in the remainder of his works.

Even without its cultural symbolism, however, *Il mistero del poeta* is the most purely romantic of all Fogazzaro's novels. Like Dante's *Vita nuova*, which it resembles in so many respects—its mixture of prose and poetry, the poet's love for the lady during her life and after her death, and even details like the use of the number nine and the lady's white dress—it is the detailed history and analysis of an emotion. Just as Dante used another lady as the "screen" behind which to conceal his love for Beatrice, so did Fogazzaro hide the identity of Felicitas Buchner behind the apparent similarity of Violet with Ellen Starbuck. Fogazzaro's style, even in the prose narration, is so lyrical as to have been described by most critics as highly musical. (We shall examine this aspect of his style in Chapter 8.) To those who consider "practical" matters—politics, ethics, morality, even religion—alien to "true" poetry, *Il mistero del poeta* should seem the most purely poetic of all Fogazzaro's novels. For those of broader vision and more catholic tastes, it remains one of his best because of the intensity of the emotions which Fogazzaro describes and the skill with which he makes them come alive for the reader.

CHAPTER 5

Italy Then and Now

I Science and (versus?) Religion

D URING and after the writing of *Il mistero del poeta*, Fogazzaro also worked on various other projects. While listening to music, he would often "translate" the impression it made on him into poetry. Several of his *Versioni dalla musica* ("Translations from Music") date from this period, as does the short story *R. Schumann (dall'op. 68)*. In the latter, a lady plays a piece from Schumann's Opus 68 and asks each guest to write a description of the scene which it suggests to him. Two of the guests describe very romantic scenes, whereas the narrator presents a farrago of nonsense. That the story is meant as a leg-pull is clear from the foolishness which the narrator produces, and also from the subject-matter, Schumann's Opus 68. This opus is a collection of short pieces entitled *Für die Jugend* "For Youth", none of whose pieces fit the description given, or would bear the description given it in the story or any of the wildly romantic interpretations placed on it.[1]

In 1887, a collection of Fogazzaro's short stories, *Fedele ed altri racconti* ("Fedele and Other Tales") appeared. He continued to write other *novelle*, of which the best is perhaps *Màlgari*,[2] a story of sixteenth-century Venice with an atmosphere like that of a fairy-tale. A foundling called Màlgari is brought up by a woman who is told in a dream that if she does not wish to lose her, she must keep her from all music and poetry. At the end of the story, after Màlgari has been carefully shielded from all contact with poetry or music, she meets a young Nordic musician, who loves her but does not dare to declare his love. Màlgari marries the Doge, and on her wedding-trip discovers that one of the sailors is the young Nordic musician. He tells her of a magnificent poem of his father-land (clearly the *Kalevala)* and recites parts of it to her. Then he plays to her, on an Italian violin, a sublime melody. After he has finished,

57

Màlgari has vanished, leaving behind nothing but a handkerchief soaked with tears.

Fogazzaro also began to give lectures, to the *Accademia Olìmpica* of Vicenza and other societies. One of his first efforts along this line was his *Un'opinione di Alessandro Manzoni* ("An opinion of Alessandro Manzoni", 1887), in which he sought to rebut Manzoni's assertion that there were enough other things in the world to write about so that love did not need to be the central theme of fiction. Fogazzaro was at this point in the midst of the composition of *Il mistero del poeta;* consequently, it was quite natural for him to defend the opposite thesis. In his last three novels, however, he seems to have come around at least partly to Manzoni's point of view.

In 1889, Fogazzaro read a book which made a very strong impression on him; the American geologist Joseph Le Conte's *Evolution and Its Relation to Religious Thought* (1888). In this work, Le Conte advanced the theory that the evolutionary hypothesis not only does not deny the assumption of a Creator, but requires it. Hence, according to Le Conte, science in no wise excludes or contradicts religion. Fogazzaro was greatly excited over the possibility of reconciling the Darwinian theory with Christian doctrine, and began to read extensively in this field. The next five years were largely devoted to assimilating current discussions of the relation of science to religion into his own thought, and to making his conclusions known. He gave three lectures, upholding the basic reconciliability of evolution with the Catholic faith, and suggesting that mankind, rather than "descending" from the ape, was "ascending" in the course of its development towards the divine. Especially important, in this connection, were his three lectures *Per un recente raffronto delle teorie di Sant'Agostino e di Darwin circa la creazione* ("On a Recent Comparison of the Theories of Saint Augustine and Darwin Concerning Creation", 1891); *Per la bellezza di un'idea* ("On the Beauty of an Idea", 1892); and *L'origine dell'uomo e il sentimento religioso* ("The Origin of Man and Religious Feeling", 1893).

The first of these lectures was delivered before a learned society, the Istituto Vèneto of Venice, and attracted little attention when it was first given. The second was given to a more popular audience, the Ateneo Vèneto (also of Venice), and was published in the *Rassegna Nazionale,* arousing considerable interest and no little discussion. Rome, not Venice, was the scene of the delivery of the third lecture. It was preceded by much excitement, and was attended by a large gathering of high-ranking members of society, including no less a personage than Queen Margherita. Fogazzaro repeated it at Naples and Milan, before equally large audiences and with great success. From this time on, Fogazzaro became a well-known public figure, with a large following, especially among society ladies—a phenomenon which did not add to the favor shown him by more intellectually pretentious circles.

After the delivery of each of these lectures, and even more after their publication as separate opuscules, Fogazzaro became embroiled in controversies over their content. He found many sympathizers among the more liberal Catholic laymen and clergy, making a number of new friends in this connection. One of the most important of these was Monsignor Giàcomo Bonomelli, bishop of Cremona, who had long been in favor of a more forward-looking and liberal attitude, especially concerning the relation between church and state. Another was Cardinal Capecelatro of Capua, also a friend of a dynamic, rather than a static, conception of modern Catholicism. On the other hand, Fogazzaro was attacked by the extremists on both sides—radical thinkers who found another target for their anticlericalism, and ultraconservative clericals (including the Vicenza newspaper *Il Berico*, which was continually girding at its fellow-Vicentine Fogazzaro). Apprehensive lest his ideas receive explicit ecclesiastical disapproval, Fogazzaro submitted his texts to authorities like Mons. Bonomelli and Cardinal Capecelatro before publishing them. He carefully avoided mentioning Rosmini's name; nevertheless, the theological aspects of his theorizing were strongly criticized by the Jesuit newspaper *Civiltà Cattolica*, especially for their implicit Rosminianism. Fogazzaro was able to escape official condemnation in connection with these lectures, but his experiences on this occasion gave him a fore-taste of later difficulties. He gave vent to his bitterness in one of his most intense poems, *Notte di passione* ("Night of Suffering," 1891), with its famous opening line *Ogni plebe m'insulta, e rossa e nera* "Every rabble insults me, both red and black."

II   Pìccolo mondo antico

In the late 1880's and early 1890's, Fogazzaro was kept very busy by his work on the relation between science and religion, and was frequently called on for commemorative articles and discourses, as when his old teacher Giàcomo Zanella died in 1888. This activity left him little time or energy to devote to his new novel. In 1887 his father Mariano died, and for a time Antonio thought of writing his biography, since he was convinced that his father had not been properly appreciated during his life-time.[3] Nothing came of this project, but he began to work again, off and on, at the *Storia quieta*, in which the hero began to assume the traits of Mariano Fogazzaro the elder. It was not until 1893, however, that Antonio returned to the task of completing the story, which he had, by this time, re-named *Piccolo mondo antico* "Little World of Yesteryear."[4] He worked intensively at it during that year and the next, despite various interruptions, completing it on December 31, 1894. It was published in November 1895.

Piccolo mondo antico opens in 1849, with the hero, Franco Maironi, and his fiancée Luisa Rigey desiring to get married, but prevented from doing so by the disapproval of his paternal grandmother, the Marchesa Maironi. They live at Oria, in Valsolda; the Marchesa, at Cressogno, farther up Lake Lugano. The Marchesa is ultraconservative, an *austriacante* or pro-Austrian,[5] and disapproves strongly of her grandson's and his friends' patriotic, anti-Austrian sympathies. She has kept secret a will whereby the Marchese, her husband, had left the Maironi estate to Franco, and has thereby been enabled to keep the estate for herself. With financial aid from Luisa's kindly and generous uncle Piero Ribera, she and Franco get married and lead a quiet existence at Oria. A child, Maria, is born to them. From her childish mispronunciation of the name of a song, *Ombretta sdegnosa del Mississipì* ("Proud little shadow of the Mississippi") which her great-uncle Piero often sings to her, she is nicknamed *Ombretta Pipì*. The Marchesa brings all her influence to bear on the Austrian authorities to make life difficult for Franco and his family, having them spied on and persecuted for their liberal opinions. One of her agents is a government official named Pasotti, who tyrannizes over his deaf wife and whom the neighbors term a *bargnìf* or "astute devil".

A sub-plot introduces the love of Professor Gilardoni, a friend of the Maironis, for Ester Bianchi, and also his possession of a copy of the Marchese's will. He informs Franco of the existence of this copy, but Franco's idealism will not allow him to take advantage of it. When Piero Ribera is, through the Marchesa's machinations, deprived of his job, Gilardoni takes matters into his own hands. He goes to see the Marchesa, but is, in his turn, persecuted by the Austrian police. He informs Luisa of the existence of the will, thereby causing a serious disagreement between husband and wife. Luisa is proud, intellectually strong, firm, and decisive, with a skeptical, materialistic outlook on religious matters. Franco is poetically and musically inclined, vacillating, idealistic, and intensely religious. Luisa urges Franco to take steps against his grandmother, but he again refuses. The split between them is so deep that Franco leaves Oria and goes to Turin, taking a poorly paid job on a newspaper. Luisa, Ombretta, and Piero Ribera remain at Oria, in worsening poverty. Primarily from a desire to see justice done, Luisa decides to face the Marchesa and force her to honor the will. Just as she is setting out, however, the women of the town call her, in terror, to come to the lifeless corpse of Ombretta, who has been drowned in the lake through the inattention of her baby-sitter. All efforts to revive Ombretta are futile.

Franco is called from Turin by telegram, and returns briefly to Oria (in secret, because he runs the risk of arrest by the Austrian police). Luisa is inconsolable, but the death of Ombretta, instead of reconciling the couple, separates them still further. Franco's religious faith upholds and strengthens him, and makes his character firmer. Luisa, on the other hand, in her skepticism and this-worldliness, has no psychological support in the face of disaster; her apparent strength of character is brittle and breaks under this extreme pressure. It takes her a long time to recover at all from the shock of Ombretta's death. For a while, she dabbles in occultism and spiritualism, attempting to get in touch with Ombretta's spirit. When even this attempt fails, she is on the brink of total collapse. Meanwhile, Gilardoni has won the love of Ester Bianchi, his successful courtship furnishing a somewhat humorous contrast to the vicissitudes of the Maironi family. The old Marchesa has a dream in which she is reproached by the ghost of Ombretta for having caused her death by defrauding her parents of their heritage.

It is now 1859. Relations between Piedmont and Austria are reaching the breaking-point; the war of liberation is imminent. Piero Ribera is seriously ill and feels the end approaching. He does not wish to die while Franco and Luisa are still separated, and therefore arranges—not without some resistance on Luisa's part—for them to meet on Isola Bella.[6] They spend one night together, and Luisa conceives again. The old Piero dies peacefully on Isola Bella; Franco returns to Turin to enroll in the Piedmontese army in the war of liberation which is just starting.

For a long time, it was thought that Fogazzaro's inspiration for the character of Franco was primarily autobiographical—that Franco's poetical and musical interests, and his indecisiveness and inability to make himself buckle down to serious work at any one thing, reflected Fogazzaro's own experiences as a young man. It is now known, however,[7] that Franco is, rather, a portrait of Mariano Fogazzaro the elder, as Antonio remembered him from the years of his own childhood and young manhood in Turin. The *Storia quieta*, which was originally intended to transmute into fictional form the story of Mariano's and Teresa's courtship and marriage, grew into *Piccolo mondo antico* through the addition of two further psychological factors. The first of these was described by Fogazzaro [8] as a conflict between husband and wife over religion and ethics, with the necessity of decision on a specific point; the second, a great unexpected sorrow which reconciles them. Franco is probably the best, though by no means the only, example of Fogazzaro's ability—which he of course shares with all great creative artists—to use his observation of a particular individual as a starting-point, and then to take the character thus portrayed into further vicissitudes and psychological development. In *Piccolo mondo antico*, Franco grows, through his sufferings, into a firmer, more decisive man. Fogazzaro makes it abundantly clear that this change is due specifically to Franco's unshakable religious faith.

The character of Luisa was drawn, not from Antonio's mother Teresa, but from an old friend of his mother, Luisa Campioni (née Venini). This lady was considerably older than Fogazzaro, having been born in 1818; but at the time in which *Piccolo mondo antico* is set, she would have been in her thirties. Antonio remembered her from that period, when he was a child and she told him fairy-stories. When her daughter Gemma died, she was unable to accept the consolations of religion that Fogazzaro urged on her, sending her a copy of the book which had brought about his own reconversion, Gratry's *Philosophie du Crédo*. She described herself as "lacking the strength to kiss the hand that had struck her".[9] On the other hand, Fogazzaro made the Luisa of the novel more proud and confident of her intellectual powers than Luisa Campioni Venini shows herself in her letters.

Of the other characters in *Piccolo mondo antico*, Fogazzaro distinguished between those who were, in the story, given their real-life names, and those who appeared under pseudonyms. In addition to a number of quite minor personages, the first category included Fogazzaro's own uncle Pietro, with the name changed only slightly, from Barrera to Ribera. The extremely sympathetic and generous character which Fogazzaro gives Piero Ribera in the novel is his homage to his mother's brother for having made Mariano's and Teresa's marriage possible. Fogazzaro goes farther and develops Piero Ribera into the guardian angel who watches over Luisa and Franco in their years of greatest sorrow, and who in the end brings them together again.

Under the second heading come a number of secondary but nevertheless important personages. Teresa Fogazzaro Barrera does appear in the novel, but in the person of Luisa's mother, Teresa Rigey. Certain aspects of the old Marchesa—her rigid authoritarianism, her hostility to liberal views, her refusal to permit Franco and Luisa to marry—reflect the relation of Antonio's paternal grandfather Giovanni Antonio to his son Mariano. Professor Gilardoni and Ester Bianchi were also drawn from friends of Fogazzaro's. Ombretta clearly reflects Fogazzaro's recollections of his own daughters and grand-daughters. Even the episode of Ombretta's drowning was based on a real event: Fogazzaro's son Mariano was nearly drowned at Oria, much to the terror of his parents and sister.[10]

The second name which Fogazzaro gave the novel, "Little World of Yesteryear," emphasizes two fundamental aspects of the tale. It portrays a microcosm, a whole world in miniature, ordinary people living ordinary lives, which Fogazzaro describes in great and (on the whole) loving detail, in an environment which he had known intimately since his earliest childhood. The novel still remained a "quiet story," in that its characters do not manifest inner ideological conflicts (as do those of *Daniele Cortis* and the later novels of the Maironi series), nor violent passions (such as we find in *Malombra* and *Il mistero del poeta*). Franco's and Luisa's emotions, in particular, are intense but not in any way melodramatic, even in the best sense of that term. The larger world exists and makes its presence felt—especially in the conflict between patriotic liberals and the Austrian authorities—but remains in the background.

Even when it appeared, *Piccolo mondo antico* was a period-piece, since it was set between forty and fifty years previous to 1895. Its time, the late Risorgimento, was already beginning to be idealized at the expense of the post-1870 period.[11] Italians of all classes were looking back on that time as one of idealism and heroism, forgetting (if they had ever known them) the divergent aims of such figures as Cavour, Garibaldi, and Mazzini, and the resultant sharp conflicts between them.[12] *Piccolo mondo antico* was therefore far less likely to arouse dissent and hostility than Fogazzaro's other novels, which were much more oriented towards contemporary life and its problems.

Fogazzaro's humor is nowhere more evident than in *Piccolo mondo antico*, in both his casual remarks concerning one character or another, and the skillful genre-portraits that he gives, especially of minor types such as priests and villagers. In many instances, this humor is manifested in their conversations, which, for the sake of realism, he reports as they would originally have taken place in Lombard (in some instances, Venetian) dialect. Earlier critics objected on puristic grounds to Fogazzaro's use of dialect, which in *Piccolo mondo antico* is more extensive than in any other of his novels. In recent decades, however, the widespread use of dialect in many neo-realistic films has rendered the general public more aware of its necessity and justification, so that its presence in Fogazzaro's novels is no longer considered as objectionable as it used to be.

Piccolo mondo antico and the three novels which followed it—*Piccolo mondo moderno*, *Il Santo* ("*The Saint*"), and *Leila*—form a tetralogy,[13] dealing with the fortunes of two generations of the Maironi family and the fate of the ideals, first of Franco and then of his son Piero. The four novels, taken together, afford a clear representation of Fogazzaro's view of the state of Italy, and his answers to its problems, especially in moral and religious matters, as follows:

> *Piccolo mondo antico:* How has Italy gotten into the state it is now in?
> *Piccolo mondo moderno:* What is wrong with present-day Italy?
> *Il santo:* What should be done to remedy Italy's troubles?
> *Leila:* When the solutions proposed have been rejected, what, if anything, can be done?

Fogazzaro's technique in answering these questions involves both direct representation and indirect reference by symbolization of cultural factors. Thus, the major characters in *Piccolo mondo antico* embody overtly the opposing forces in the Risorgimento. The old Marchesa represents the conservative, *austriacante* aristocracy. Several of the petty officials who were subservient to the conservatives, such as the *bargnìf* Pasotti, are represented among the minor characters. Franco and Luisa are the younger, progressive and liberal, independent-minded generation.

Beyond this level, however, we may well identify Franco and Luisa with two major aspects of the Italian inheritance. Franco symbolizes the restless, self-doubting force of intellectually-oriented religion.[14] Luisa stands for the superficially firmer but psychologically more brittle force of reason and hence of rationalism. From the union of these two, results of great beauty and significance might be expected, and their first fruits are symbolized by Ombretta Pipì, one of the most immediately appealing characters in modern Italian literature. It is noteworthy that, in the Maironi tetralogy, several characters die in childhood or in youth: Ombretta, Franco Maironi's wife Elisa, Franco-Benedetto himself, and (between the action of *Il santo* and that of *Leila*) Lelia Camin's fiancé Andrea. In each instance, the death of one of these characters symbolizes the dashing of hopes, and the subsequent action of the over-all story is radically re-oriented in consequence.

In the immediate context of *Piccolo mondo antico*, Ombretta of course embodies Franco's and Luisa's hopes for the future, and every reader sympathizes with their loss and feels with them that their hopes have been dashed. But in the development of the story, her death is, when looked at superficially, unmotivated: why should it come at the particular point it does? The answer is that the seemingly unmotivated death of Ombretta has symbolic function, representing the loss of the best results that should have come in the nineteenth century from the fusion of the emotional, religious, and rational elements in the Italian tradition. The ultimate responsibility for her death of course rests with the old Marchesa, who had, through her rejection of Franco and Luisa, failed to take adequate care and provide for the upbringing of the little Maria, just as the conservative aristocracy of the time had, in the view liberals like Fogazzaro, rejected the vital, life-giving part of their cultural heritage. The immediate responsibility, that of the woman to whose care Ombretta had been entrusted and who had failed to look after her properly, is also symbolic of the incapacity of the Italian lower classes in the first half of the nineteenth century to care properly for their cultural heritage and its fruits. After the death of Ombretta, a new heir will have to be begotten to continue the Maironi line, just as a new effort had to be made in the late Risorgimento to bring fresh fruits from the national culture after the first fine hopes had faded.

By almost unanimous agreement among both the general public and literary critics, *Piccolo mondo antico* is customarily regarded as the summit of Fogazzaro's literary achievement. There are several reasons for this opinion. Some are negative: almost alone among his novels, *Piccolo mondo antico* is devoid of both polemic elements and strong erotic passions. It is set in an epoch generally regarded as near enough to be still meaningful to modern readers, and yet distant enough to be romantic and looked back upon with nostalgia. In the late Risorgimento, the choices that successful unification was to force upon the nation were still open. After a given situation has developed (such as what many persons regarded as the undesirable turn that matters took after 1870 in Italy), it is possible to look back and engage in wishful thinking about the time before the "wrong" choices were made, and about "the road not taken".[15]

On the positive side, readers can empathize strongly with both Franco and Luisa, recognizing them both as full and rich personalities, each with great merits but near-tragic faults.[16] A host of secondary and minor characters, and a wealth of detail, make the reader feel that he has come to know an entire community in its historical setting, and has lived with it through all the different types of experience—petty and important, humorous and serious—that constitute its life. At the same time, Fogazzaro awakens our warm sympathy, so that we finish *Piccolo mondo antico* with a mixture of sadness and pleasure, but without strong partisan feelings aroused either for or against the author's opinions.

III   *International Fame*

At the beginning of 1895, after finishing the writing of *Piccolo mondo antico*, Fogazzaro returned to Rome to deliver a two-part lecture, this time on *I misteri dello spìrito umano e la scienza* ("The Mysteries of the Human Spirit and Science"). He gave it on January 24 and February 2 to a full audience, of whom many were members of elegant society. Queen Margherita attended both talks; this was the first of several occasions on which she manifested esteem for him and his works.

After his return to Vicenza, and while he was correcting the proofs of *Piccolo mondo antico*, Fogazzaro suffered the heaviest emotional blow of his life. His dearly beloved son Mariano, who had been studying at Padua, came home unexpectedly on May 2, 1895, and, after a two-week illness, died on May 16. For a time, the grief-stricken Antonio withdrew from almost all contacts outside his family. Soon, however, he resumed his normal activities, and in fact returned to the fray in connection with Antonio Rosmini and the problems of Catholicism. He contributed an article to a volume commemorating the hundredth anniversary of Rosmini's birth, and also a more popularizing (and more polemical) article to the magazine *La Nuova Antologia ("The New Anthology")*.[17]

The immediate popularity of *Piccolo mondo antico* brought Fogazzaro fame both in Italy and abroad. *Piccolo mondo antico* was translated into French, English, and other languages, arousing interest in his earlier works and causing them to be translated as well. On October 25, 1896, he was named Senator.[18] Because he was not rich enough, the decree could not be confirmed by the Senate until his possessions and the tax based thereon had reached the necessary minimum. Confirmation of his nomination as Senator was therefore delayed until April of 1900.

Foreign visitors, especially French, began to seek him out at his home in Vicenza.[19] He was invited to Paris to inaugurate the second year's cycle of lectures given under the auspices of the recently founded but highly prestigious Société des Conférences. In March of 1898 he visited Paris for the first time, speaking on March 8 on the topic *Le grand poète de l'avenir* ("The Great Poet of the Future"). The sentiments voiced in the lecture were noble—hope for poetry as an expression of a religious and at the same time evolutionary conception of the universe, proclaiming the loftiest human ideals and goals—but unfortunately not prophetic of the course twentieth-century poetry was to take.

Two further lectures, one at Venice on March 22 on *Scienza e dolore* ("Science and Sorrow") and one at Rome on March 31 on *Il progresso in relazione della felicità* ("Progress in Relation to Happiness"), continued Fogazzaro's discussions of evolution in relation to religion and poetry. These and preceding lectures on this topic were published in the same year in a volume entitled *Ascensioni umane* ("Human Ascents"). The relation between the theory of evolution and Catholic dogma had been the subject of increasing controversy during the 1890's. A book on *Evolution and Dogma* by an American priest, Father John Augustine Zahm, had been published in an Italian translation but withdrawn from circulation for fear of official condemnation.[20] Despite a certain amount of hostile criticism from intransigent ultraconservatives, Fogazzaro's *Ascensioni umane* were not condemned. As frequently happens with famous men in their later years, collections of his earlier works began to appear: a volume of Fogazzaro's *Poesie scelte* ("Selected Poems") and one containing his *Discorsi* ("Discourses") were published in 1898.

IV   Piccolo mondo moderno

Fogazzaro began to write the immediate sequel to *Piccolo mondo antico* in 1897. As might be expected in view of his multifarious activities in the final years of the century, his work on the new novel was slow and intermittent. It was finished in 1900, with the title *Piccolo mondo moderno* "Little World of Nowadays." It was first published in serial form in the *Nuova Antologia* between December 16, 1900, and March 16, 1901, appearing as a book in the following month.

We learn, in the course of the story, of certain events which the novelist has imagined as taking place between the end of *Piccolo mondo antico* and its sequel. Franco Maironi was seriously wounded in the war in 1859, and returned home to die in 1860. Luisa also died soon after giving birth to her son Piero. The latter has been brought up by the Marchese and Marchesa Scremin in the petty, narrow-minded, ultraclerical atmosphere of a small city in the Vèneto (obviously Vicenza). Piero has been torn, in the course of growing up, between mystical religiosity and carnal sensuality. He has yielded to the latter only once (as Fogazzaro himself had done in his youth), and has sought relief for his desires by marrying his foster-parents' daughter Elisa Scremin. She, however, went insane soon after her marriage, and, at the opening of the novel, is in an asylum near Brescia.

Piero is active in politics and is elected mayor of his city. His politics—liberal, socially oriented Catholicism—cause him trouble with the clericalist majority in the municipal administration. A beautiful young woman, Jeanne Dessalle, who is separated from her husband, is living near the city in the elegant Villa Diedo, together with her aesthetically-minded, affected brother Carlino Dessalle. She loves Piero, but does not desire sexual intercourse with him, having acquired a repugnance for coitus from her unhappy marriage. Piero is strongly attracted to her on a physical basis, but resists temptation. Ever since his boyhood, he has felt a strong urge to become a Benedictine monk, especially when he visits the old monastery at Praglia.[21] His confessor, the wise old priest Don Giuseppe Flores, advises Piero not to go into a monastery, but to continue in his present position, trusting in Providence.

On a visit to Praglia, Piero finds Jeanne there and is troubled by her presence, but she persuades him to continue in a Platonic relationship. His clerical antagonists in the municipal government are scandalized by his apparent liaison with Jeanne. They plan to entrap him in an administrative scandal, but Piero forestalls them by resigning. Jeanne gives a party at Villa Diedo, with musical entertainment provided by Maestro Chieco, Carlino, and others. Piero tries to seduce Jeanne, but her repugnance for sexual intercourse saves them from becoming lovers. Piero toys with the idea of giving away his possessions in the Vèneto—which his ancestors had amassed in ways which he considers unethical—and going to live quietly in his parents' house at Oria. Jeanne persuades Piero to visit the hotel at Vena di Fonte Alta, in the hills above the city, where she and Carlino are staying. There, Piero finds rivals for Jeanne's favors. She finally indicates that she is willing to become his mistress, and he is just on the point of tip-toeing down the hall-way to her room, when he receives a letter from his mother-in-law announcing that his wife is on the point of death, and summoning him to her side.

Piero finds Elisa still alive with her reason miraculously restored; she dies comforted by Christian faith. His mystical impulses prevail and, with the consent of Don Giuseppe Flores, Piero decides to leave the secular world and enter into some, as yet unspecified kind of ascetic life.

Even while the novel was appearing in the *Nuova Antologia*, its readers were struck and not wholly pleased by the difference between *Piccolo mondo antico* and its sequel.[22] There were two chief reasons for this reaction. In the first place, *Piccolo mondo moderno* deals, not with an already somewhat remote and idealized period and stage in Italian history, but with contemporary life, which Fogazzaro described with his customary ability to portray and satirize all too effectively. His description of the petty intrigues and the bigotry of small-city ultraconservatives was extremely detailed and accurate, based as it was on his many years of experience of life in Vicenza and contact with its politics. The sordid and often drab realities of modern existence were far less attractive as subjects of phantasy—which, after all, is for many readers the main reason for reading a novel[23]—than the half-legendary days of the Risorgimento.

The other main cause of readers' dissatisfaction with *Piccolo mondo moderno* was the character of Piero. Even more than Daniele Cortis, he seemed to many—especially masculine—readers to be considerably less than the ideal hero. Even his father, Franco Maironi, had at least gone off, in the end, to fight like a man for his country. Piero's inner doubts, hesitations, and torments, and his constant battle against carnal temptation awoke but little response in the ordinary novel-reader, conditioned ever since the time of Boccaccio and the *Novellino* to expect the hero of a story to be aggressively male, particularly in sexual prowess. It has become customary, especially among Italian literary critics, to speak of Fogazzaro's men as "weak" and of his women as "strong," primarily on the basis of the amount of emotional stress they undergo.

Such an interpretation, however, rests on a superficial identification of strength of character with "determination" as manifested in unhesitating, apparently secure action, reflecting an essentially egoistic attitude towards one's relation to others. For Fogazzaro, on the other hand, strength of character is altruistic rather than egoistic. It is attained only as a result of internal struggle towards lofty goals and victory over one's baser self, even at the cost of physical health. Piero, we must not forget, is quite successful in dealing with the affairs of the world; he is good enough to be mayor of the city for a year, and to do an obviously satisfactory job until he is forced out of his position by intrigue. Yet he must set his sights on higher goals. Through the vicissitudes of his relationship with Jeanne, Piero finally develops his strength of character to the point where, after his wife's death, he takes the decisive step of cutting his ties with the world and starts to follow his vocation for monastic life.

Piero, drawn from no one specific prototype but undoubtedly reflecting (and going far beyond) much of Fogazzaro's own inner agonizing, was much less immediately appealing than Jeanne. Feminine readers, especially, tended to identify themselves with her, in her *fin-de-siècle* beauty, elegance, frigidity, and slight eccentricity.[24] Fogazzaro had met, in 1887, the twenty-two-year-old Yole Moschini Biaggini, with whom he was very much taken. She had flirted with him to a certain extent, trying to excite his interest by unmotivated contradictions and provocations in their conversation.[25] As came to be his habit with more than one beautiful young woman, Fogazzaro attempted (in this case unsuccessfully) to convert the somewhat skeptical Yole to his brand of religion, while himself remaining free of emotional involvement. She seems to have had a somewhat more complicated attitude towards him, especially on the occasion of a casual meeting with him at the monastery of Praglia.[26] Both before and after the publication of *Piccolo mondo antico*, there was uninformed gossip about the

relationship of Fogazzaro and the signora Moschini. As in other instances (notably those of Felicitas Buchner and Miss Starbuck),
Fogazzaro sublimated his emotions in his creative writing, going far
beyond anything that he may have said or done in real life.[27]

Fogazzaro's mouth-piece for his own opinions concerning religion
in *Piccolo mondo moderno* is the old priest Don Giuseppe Flores,
whose real-life original was the author's uncle Don Giuseppe Fogazzaro. He is a model of kindness, charity, and human sympathy, giving Piero comfort and solace in the latter's moments of despair. In
Chapter II, when Piero feels that God has deserted him, Don
Giuseppe replies:

> First of all, don't be so afraid of your temptations! Don't think that you
> are tempted very much more than so many others who may seem to you
> secure from evil, all God's people. Your temptations against faith, for that
> matter, even though you don't resist them greatly, don't seem to me to be
> feared. [. . .] Just look how small these difficulties are. God doesn't help
> you? What do you mean, He doesn't help you? He permits you to be
> tempted, but then, when you fought, as you told me, when you were vic-
> torious, as you said to me, Who breathed into you the effective strength?
> God works in secret; we cannot sense what He performs in us and outside of
> us, but neither can we overcome the flesh without His help. If, once, He
> did permit you to fall, He then raised you up again immediately.

In the same chapter, when Piero is not yet ready for a definitive
renunciation of the world, Don Giuseppe advises him to stay in it,
resigning the mayoralty if necessary, and urges him to seek God in
the "monastery cell" of his inmost heart:

> My dear man, it is necessary to stay in the world and it is necessary to
> leave it. Your cell must be in your heart, in the innermost part of your
> heart. Yes, dear man, weep for sorrow, but weep also for tenderness. There
> is Some-one who is preparing the cell for you at this moment, who is ready
> to wait for you there, who is telling you to come to Him, to rest your head
> on His bosom because He has so much pity for you, because He wishes to
> pardon you for everything, everything, everything. Go in, go in, don't
> resist. Do you say that you feel so badly? Yes, because you are looking at
> the worldly things to which you are attached, and Jesus is in them too, but a
> severe Jesus, a sad Jesus, and nothing makes the heart ache as much as the
> severe and sad look of Jesus. [. . .] How could you live in such a torment,
> how could you fail to turn from Jesus in his severity to Jesus in his love?

Don Giuseppe, in his Christian charity and understanding
kindness, directed more by feelings of love for his fellow-man than

by externals of dogma or observances, is Fogazzaro's ideal priest. Flores' very undogmatic and unclerical approach to problems of conscience made him the object of condemnation from many critics, both clerical and literary, who found its emotional basis hard to accept.

The other outstanding personage of *Piccolo mondo moderno* is Piero's mother-in-law, the Marchesa Nene Scremin. She appears at the beginning of the novel as simply a stingy old lady who raises a fuss over an egg which has disappeared. As the story proceeds, however, we see her in a very different light. She seems to be indifferent to all that does not concern her directly, but in actuality she has a firm, strong mind with well-considered opinions. The Marchesa is devoted to the well-being of her family and of Piero. In her loving care for her daughter and her son-in-law, she functions as a link between the outer world—as represented by the society of Vicenza—and the inner drama of Piero, Elisa, and Jeanne.[28] The scene of the Marchesa's conversation with Don Giuseppe, in which the two old people express their concern for the well-being of her daughter and son-in-law, is one of the most moving Fogazzaro ever wrote. The relation of Piero to his mother-in-law closely parallels that of Fogazzaro himself to Rita's mother, the Countess Valmarana, from whom the Marchesa was principally drawn.

One of the implications of the adjective *moderno* in the title of this novel is the contrast between the narrow, backward, closed society of a small Italian city like Vicenza, and the *fin-de-siècle* elegance and modernity of foreigners like Jeanne and her brother Carlino. The latter is presented in a rather unfavorable light, as being affected and dilettantish in his aesthetic pretensions, despite his wide knowledge of contemporary and earlier culture. He and the eccentric, though rather more likeable, 'cellist Maestro Chieco organize musicales at Villa Diedo, and he shares Fogazzaro's own enthusiasm for the "musica antica" of the eighteenth century. Carlino was drawn primarily from a Florentine, the cosmopolitan aristocrat Carlo Placci, whose novel *Il furto* ("The Theft") Fogazzaro considered the best Italian portrayal of elegant international society.[29] Fogazzaro purposely gave his Carlino some unamiable traits, both to differentiate him from Carlo Placci and to emphasize the contrast between Jeanne and her brother. Chieco was, as we already know, the Milanese 'cellist Gaetano Braga.

In addition to the city itself, in which every-one recognized Vicenza immediately when the novel was published, the remaining background of the story can be easily identified. Villa Diedo was obviously the Villa Valmarana at Velo d'Àstico, north of Vicenza, even to its cube-like shape and its frescoes painted by Tièpolo. Fonte di Vena Alta is the Alpine resort of Tonezza del Cimone, in the valley of the Àstico somewhat beyond Velo. Oria and the Valsolda keep reappearing, as the place to which Piero yearns to retreat—that is, to his parents' house where he can find spiritual peace and freedom from his inner conflicts. In just the same way, many Italians of the post-Risorgimento wished they could return to the "little world of yesteryear" of their parents.

Why Oria and the Valsolda, however? Was it necessary for *Piccolo mondo moderno* to be tied in with *Piccolo mondo antico?* It has been suggested[30] that this connection was unnecessary: that Fogazzaro's new hero might just as well have been the son of other parents than Franco and Luisa Maironi. To understand the reason for Piero's relationship to them, we must again turn to the broader symbolism of the story. Franco and Luisa stand for a whole generation, that of the late Risorgimento. The next generation, living thirty or thirty-five years later, were the spiritual and psychological children of the earlier, carrying on under new and different circumstances, and confronting difficulties which had arisen out of the conditions which their parents' generation had helped to create. From the union of Franco's and Luisa's characteristics in Piero, we are to understand that Piero continues their heritage as the representative of his entire age-group.

Fogazzaro's basic purpose in *Piccolo mondo moderno* was to exemplify, through Piero Maironi and his environment, what was wrong with the Italy of his time. So far as the actual setting itself was concerned—including the intellectual and religious backwardness of the population and their local government—a direct portrayal was all that was necessary. Why, however, should Piero have been enamored of a foreign woman? Why should his wife, an Italian, have been out of the picture, deranged and in an asylum, for nearly the whole length of the story? Elisa's incapacitation symbolizes clearly the unfruitfulness of the late nineteenth-century Italian cultural life, and its inability to give satisfaction to those who had high aspirations for the betterment of Italy. Piero's interest in Jeanne also symbolizes the temptation for the sensitive Italian to replace his unsatisfactory, intellectually bankrupt modern culture for the attractions of a more up-to-date foreign civilization.

In the next-to-the-last chapter of *Piccolo mondo moderno*, after

Elisa has died, the director of the asylum speaks to Don Giuseppe
Flores, expressing his concern over what seems to him to be Piero's
abnormal behavior in the chapel of the institution. The director
regards Piero as an incipient religious maniac because the latter
groans and fixes a hallucinated gaze on the crucifix:

"You may tell me that the saints, too, did things like that. I respect the
saints, I don't want to bring even Saint Teresa into the discussion; but do
you think that there still are saints? I doubt it! Nowadays there is hysteria
and there is religious mania. For me, this morning's acts were those
characteristic of religious mania. It may well be that they will remain
within certain limits of time and restraint, but it may also happen that they
will develop farther. And now you understand why I have said what I have
said. I really feel that I have fulfilled a duty."

"Eh!" said Don Giuseppe, sadly, with his head bowed, like one who,
concerning a serious matter, neither has nor can have the certainty that he
would wish for, but would be inclined to a different opinion from the one
which is making him thoughtful. "Thank you."

Toward the very end of the book, Don Giuseppe, writing to the
Marchesa, indicates that he has had his doubts as to the desirability
of Piero's embracing a state of absolute poverty and penitence,
saying: "I confess, indeed, that perhaps, in view of his ability, his
culture, his social standing and this unexpected return to the Christian faith [. . .] I would have desired of him an active participation
in public life, also for the especial good of this poor country of ours.
I soon recognized that Piero's resolution was unshakable, nor would
I now be sure that, if I were to oppose it, I would be doing the
proper thing."

The difference between the attitudes of the director of the
asylum and Don Flores makes clear the two ways that Italians might
regard Piero's action. The director is intelligent and cultured, and
represents the view-point of an educated Italian psychologist. Don
Giuseppe disagrees with him, since he has a different outlook on
religious inspiration. Inasmuch as Don Flores represents, in general,
Fogazzaro's own opinion, we are to assume that the author intends
us to sympathize with Piero and accept the priest's rather than the
psychologist's diagnosis.

Fogazzaro's message in *Piccolo mondo moderno* is that a
progressive, liberal Christian approach to the problems of modern
life, in the microcosm of the small city, is doomed to failure. A
revival of religious feeling, symbolized by Piero's decision to aban-

don politics and secular life, will be needed, at least on the part of some, to bring about the needed regeneration. Yet there remained a dilemma as to how such a Christian orientation would be interpreted. The only type of religious revival that Italians have known, ever since the Middle Ages, has been the intensely other-worldly, self-abasing, masochistic mysticism of the Umbrian flagellants and similar groups.[31] If Fogazzaro had had Piero remain politically active in the community, showing at the same time an intensely religious spirit, his readers would have regarded Piero as a self-seeking hypocrite. On the other hand, a purely ascetic Piero oriented exclusively towards religious evangelism—which was the only type of convert that would seem realistic to an Italian reader—would by many be interpreted as a fanatic, a madman. Fogazzaro chose the latter alternative, as we shall see in discussing *Il santo.* By introducing the director of the asylum to present the "man of the world's" diagnosis, however, Fogazzaro showed his awareness of this problem, which has remained to beset almost all discussions of his last three novels.

Piccolo mondo moderno has, in general, been regarded as inferior to its immediate predecessor, a let-down from Fogazzaro's peak of creative inspiration. This opinion does not stem from the usual objection to sequels, that they merely repeat the same formula which led to the success of the first book of a series.[32] It is due, rather, to several basic features of *Piccolo mondo moderno* which are different from those of *Piccolo mondo antico.* The former deals with the "unromantic" post-Risorgimento, and with every-day small-city life. It is strongly satirical, especially of Fogazzaro's *bête noire*, reactionary clericalism. For some readers, probably the novel's worst fault is that Piero loves God and religion more than he does Jeanne, and in the end he does not go to bed with her. The over-all atmosphere of the novel is one of dissatisfaction with existing situations, in both private and public life. At the end the reader is left, not with an optimistic conclusion like that of *Daniele Cortis,* nor even with a specifically pessimistic conclusion, but with no conclusion at all. Real life is this way, but most novels are not. Piero simply disappears, and neither the characters nor the reader know what is to become of him. In a novel of suspense, the reader is conditioned to accept a conclusion in which some expectations are intentionally left unfulfilled ("continued in the next installment"). *Piccolo mondo moderno,* however, is not a novel of suspense.

Taken in and for itself, and viewed objectively apart from

culturally conditioned attitudes and expectations, *Piccolo mondo moderno* is a much better book than it is usually considered to be. It is well constructed, and keeps the reader's interest through lively and often amusing dialogue. Many of its episodes are particularly evocative and remain in the reader's memory, for instance Piero's and Jeanne's encounters at Villa Diedo and at Fonte di Vena Alta, or the conversation between the Marchesa and Don Giuseppe. Less romantic, but equally memorable, are Fogazzaro's satirical descriptions of the machinations of the anti-Maironi cabal in the municipal government. More subject to individual readers' pro- or anti-religious reactions are the descriptions of Piero's mystical experiences and visions; but their effectiveness cannot be denied, nor can that of the novel as a whole, as a description of *fin-de-siècle* life in a small north Italian city like Vicenza.

CHAPTER 6

Is Reform Possible?

I *Modernism*

A S the new century opened, Fogazzaro—now fifty-eight years old and at the height of his fame—was very busy with a number of different activities. Collections of his earlier works were appearing, for instance a third volume of short stories, *Idillii spezzati* ("Broken Idylls," 1901) and a volume of minor essays and speeches (*Minime*, 1901). He was very much in demand as a speaker and lecturer. Fogazzaro had also been encouraged by various friends to try his hand at writing drama, ever since the famous actress Eleonora Duse had discussed with him, in 1886, the possibility of making *Daniele Cortis* into a stage-play.[1] Fogazzaro's few and quite unsuccessful attempts at play-writing date from the first years of the twentieth century. *El garòfolo rosso* ("The Red Carnation," a one-act play in Venetian dialect) was published in 1901 and performed in 1902; it was a failure because of its excessive realism. *Nadejde* and *Il ritratto mascherato* ("The Masked Portrait"), both dating from 1902, were no more successful.

Much more important, from the point of view of Fogazzaro's development, were his relations with the increasingly active group of would-be reformers in the Roman Catholic church, known collectively as "Modernists." Under this over-all label were grouped a number of thinkers of rather different orientations. Those with whom Fogazzaro had the most contact were the Italian-English Baron von Hügel,[2] the French theologian-scholar Loisy,[3] the Irish Jesuit Tyrrell,[4] and the Italian priest Ròmolo Murri.[5] Loisy's main activity lay in the field of Biblical criticism, on a rather more scholarly level than that of the other three, who were primarily concerned with the effect of modern thought on Catholicism as it affected the majority of the lay believers. All of them, however, had a common interest in reconciling, if possible, the findings of modern science, in such fields as biology and textual criticism of the Bible, with the official dogmas of the Catholic church.[6] Such efforts met with considerable sympathy from a number of high-ranking prelates, including Fogazzaro's friends Mons. Bonomelli of Cremona and Cardinal Capecelatro of Capua, and also the bishop of Bèrgamo, Mons. Radini-Tedeschi. The last-mentioned had as his secretary, from 1905 to 1914, a young priest named Àngelo Roncalli.

After his nomination to the rank of senator was confirmed in 1900, Fogazzaro's visits to Rome became inevitably more frequent, and he was active in the Senate, serving on several commissions. On these occasions, he frequented the meetings of "modernist" sympathizers at the home of Pio Molajoni, in Piazza Rondanini.[7] The discussions there dealt, not so much with specific points of theology, as with problems affecting the political and social commitments of Catholics, and the internal reform of the church. As long as Leo XIII was pope, these and similar gatherings did not meet with official disapproval. After the death of Leo XIII in 1903, the new pope, Pius X, proved to be much less tolerant, and from that time on the meetings of "modernist" groups came to be regarded with hostility and even suspicion by the conservative elements in the church at Rome.

A preliminary indication of the direction that matters were to take was given in December, 1903, when five books by Loisy were put on the Index Expurgatorius.[8] A journal named *Rinnovamento* ("Renewal") was founded in Milan in 1907, and continued publication for three years, until the end of 1909. Fogazzaro was one of its contributors, but was not actively involved in determining its policy, which was one of open-minded receptivity to new ideas and outlooks.[9] Violent attacks against the journal and against Fogazzaro, Tyrrell, von Hügel, and others appeared in the official Vatican newspaper, the *Osservatore Romano*, in May of the same year. A papal decree entitled *Lamentabili sane exitu* condemned sixty-five propositions allegedly drawn from "modernist" writings. Storm-clouds seemed to be gathering, harbingers of a lightning-bolt of official condemnation. In considerable anxiety over possible developments, a group of the leading Modernists gathered for a conference at Molveno at the end of August, 1907. Fogazzaro was present, more as an observer and well-wisher than as an active participant. There was considerable discussion, but no positive conclusions were reached. On September 8, a papal encyclical entitled *Pascendi gregis* was issued, condemning en bloc all efforts at reconciling modern developments with official Catholic dogma. At the time, this condemnation was regarded as definitive, and the "modernist" movement ceased to have any importance or influence for over fifty years. Its members continued to regard themselves as devout Catholics, obedient to papal decree, even when, like Loisy and Tyrrell, they were officially excommunicated.

II   Il santo

It was against the background of the growing storm over Modernism that Fogazzaro wrote the third novel of the Maironi tetralogy, *Il santo* ("The Saint"). He began work on it in 1903, and completed it two years later; it was published in November of 1905. It continues the story of Piero Maironi after he has left his native north Italian city to devote himself to a religious life.

The opening episode of *Il santo* takes place three years after Piero's disappearance. Jeanne Dessalle is in Belgium, at Bruges, still madly in love with Piero and desirous of seing him again. A young Belgian woman, a Protestant friend of Jeanne's named Noemi d'Arxel, has heard of a Benedictine monk at Subiaco,[10] Don Clemente, who seems to resemble Maironi. Noemi's sister Maria has converted herself to Catholicism and has entered into a *mariage blanc* with an old Catholic theologian, Giovanni Selva, who is described as "the most legitimate representative of Catholic progressivism." The Selvas live in a villa near Subiaco. One evening a group of guests meet at the Selvas' to discuss the problems of Catholicism and modern knowledge. The discussion is lively, but ends inconclusively, with no concrete result. Noemi and Jeanne arrive from Belgium just as the meeting is ending. Selva tries to keep Jeanne from seeing Don Clemente; the latter, however, tries to keep her from seeing the monastery gardener, who has come with him. Jeanne sees both the priest and the gardener, and recognizes Piero, not in the former, but in the latter.

Piero has become a lay brother, under the name of Benedetto, devoting himself to the humblest of tasks, in poverty and prayer. His inner peace is such that he is not disturbed by Jeanne's reappearance. He obtains the permission of the abbot to don the garb of a Benedictine convert. In this garb, he meets Jeanne, and is interested only in her reconversion to religious faith. On learning that she has not yet recovered faith, he dismisses her with a promise that they will meet again at some later time. The abbot has been keeping the Roman ecclesiastical authorities informed of what has been going on at the Selvas'. There ensue a series of persecutions directed against Giovanni Selva and the "progressives." Benedetto is forced to give up his Benedictine garb, and goes to the small village of Jenne.[11]

At Jenne, Benedetto devotes himself to the well-being of the villagers. Sunk in age-old superstition, the inhabitants of Jenne look upon Benedetto as a "saint" (whence the title of the book), and ascribe certain healings to his miraculous abilities as a wonder-worker. He tries to disillusion them, but they will not believe his denials. On a later occasion, they expect a miracle from him, which is not forthcoming. The villagers turn against him and drive him out in disgrace.

Benedetto then goes to Rome, where he becomes the talk of the town because of his preaching a simple gospel of love and reconciliation, joined with open-mindedness and social justice. At a meeting in a home in Via della Vite, he is listened to, not only by Giovanni Selva and like-minded persons, but by a large number of elegant ladies who crowd in to hear him. Despite his popularity, however, his real message is not heeded; it is evident that he has been simply the latest fad.

The authorities in the Vatican have become greatly disturbed by Benedetto's popularity, and begin to take measures aimed at getting him out of Rome. He is able to arrange a private interview with the Pope, whom he sermonizes on the ills of the church. According to Benedetto, there are four evil spirits besetting the church, those of falsehood, clerical domination, greed, and immobility. The Pope, in his feeble reply, points out the need of prudence and his own inability to implement change due to age and incapacitation.

The Vatican authorities and the government, although nominally at odds with each other, are under the surface sufficiently in cahoots so that Benedetto is arrested after his interview with the Pope. He is taken to the office of the Minister of the Interior, who receives another sermon. Benedetto tells the Minister in no uncertain terms what is wrong with Italy. His message is essentially the same as that of Daniele Cortis, accusing the rulers of Italy of corruption and failure to allow Christian ideals to influence their actions. Benedetto is ordered to leave Rome, but instead he goes into half-hiding, living in the slum quarter of the Testaccio and ministering to the poor.

Benedetto has for some time been aware that his health is failing, due to his fasting and self-inflicted penitence. As his end approaches, he is taken to a friend's house on the Aventine, just above the Testaccio. As he is on his death-bed, both the poor from the slums and his well-to-do friends gather around him. Noemi d'Arxel becomes a convert to Catholicism; Jeanne recovers her faith. Benedetto receives the sacraments and dies in the odor of sanctity.

The first two novels of the tetralogy were essentially realistic portrayals of events that, although fictional, might well have taken place. *Il santo*, on the other hand, has much more the character of a phantasy—a vision of what Fogazzaro would have considered the way to point out a solution for the problems presented in the two preceding novels. His original intention was to call this story *La visione* ("The Vision"),[12] which would have given a better idea of the book's content and might have saved Fogazzaro some of the trouble which the title *Il santo* brought upon him.[13] In *Il santo*, Fogazzaro is essentially imagining what would happen if a man like Piero Maironi were to take literally Christ's injunction "Go and sell what you have and give it to the poor, and come and follow me",[14] and then were to attempt to minister to and reform the Italy of the turn of the century. *Il santo* is primarily a novel of ideas, and only secondarily one of character or of manners.

Benedetto, as Fogazzaro portrays him, combines the asceticism and self-immolation of a mediaeval mystic with the love of his fellow-men manifested by, say, Saint Francis of Assisi, and the direct outspokenness of a Saint Catherine of Siena or a Savonarola. It is the last-mentioned quality which has rendered the character of Benedetto unacceptable to many critics and (naturally) caused *Il santo* to be regarded with especial disfavor in reactionary ecclesiastical circles. Fogazzaro drew Benedetto principally from George Tyrrell, putting in his mouth even certain specific metaphors which Tyrrell, was in the habit of using.[15] Benedetto's populistic sympathies, and his ministry among the peasants of Jenne and the poor of the Testaccio quarter, are drawn from Don Romolo Murri.

The vicissitudes and eventual fate of Benedetto, in his apostolate, epitomize the difficulties that Fogazzaro envisaged as confronting any lay person—note that Benedetto is still a layman, not in clerical orders—who might undertake to bring Italian Catholicism to an awareness of the need for reform. Age-old superstition among the peasantry, mundane faddishness among the well-to-do, corruption in the government, and the four "evil spirits" in the church—all these stand in Benedetto's way and render his efforts futile. It would be, according to *Il santo*, a highly desirable development if the leaders of Italian religious and political life (symbolized by Piero-Benedetto in his activity on the grass-roots level) would turn their backs on the corruption of politics, on the allurements of sex and of foreign culture (Jeanne Dessalle) and would devote themselves to sincere, selfless efforts to reform the spiritual life of Italy and the Roman church from the inside. Non-Catholic Christianity is represented by Noemi d'Arxel; her conversion to the Roman church at the end of the novel tells us that Fogazzaro hoped, as a result of the type of reforms embodied in Benedetto's preaching, for the return of Protestantism to the Roman fold. All these hopes were of course an unrealistic dream on Fogazzaro's part, as subsequent events proved; but its lack of short-term reality hardly diminishes its importance as an expression of a long-term desire.

The central episode of, not only *Il santo*, but the entire Maironi tetralogy is Benedetto's interview with the Pope. The four "evil spirits" which he identifies as characterizing the current situation in the church are clearly the same as four out of the five which Rosmini had identified over half a century earlier. (The fifth, temporal rule, had disappeared when Rome became part of united Italy in 1870.) The Pope of Benedetto's interview is not Leo XIII or Pius X, but simply an abstraction representing the papacy in the conditions of those days. Fogazzaro was thoroughly justified in leaving up in the air the solution of the problems raised by Benedetto in his harangues to the Pope and the Minister of the Interior, as the history of the following half-century and more has shown.

There is an interesting parallel between *Il santo* and a work by a German author, written nearly sixty years later—Rolf Hochhuth's *Der Stellvertreter* ('The Deputy'', 1963).[16] In both of these works, an intensely devout young Italian Catholic, deeply concerned over the failure of his church and especially of the Pope to play a satisfactory rôle in the life of his times, attempts to bring about a radical change of direction and improvement by speaking directly to the Pope. His protestations are unsuccessful; soon thereafter he offers himself as a sacrifice and dies. The surface dissimilarities between the two works are of course great. Hochhuth, in his play, accuses Pope Pacelli (Pius XII) of having failed, out of fear of Russia and concern over the Vatican's investments, to halt the Nazis' campaign of extermination against the Jews.[17] His protagonist, Don Riccardo Fontana, is a Jesuit whereas Benedetto is, for a time, only a lay brother. Hochhuth's Pacelli is a person who really existed, and whom Hochhuth believed to have been self-seeking, cold, and cynically calculating.[18] Fogazzaro's Pope, on the other hand, knows perfectly well that many things are wrong, but (as he admits) he is too old, tired, and ill to be firm or effective in stamping out abuses, even if he dared. Yet there is a basic similarity between Hochhuth's and Fogazzaro's views of the moral weakness of the papacy and the church. Fontana's accusations, in *Der Stellvertreter*, can be reduced to the same four points that Benedetto makes in his sermon to the Pope concerning the "evil spirits" dominating the church of his time.

Considered simply as a story, without regard to the ideas presented therein, *Il santo* is as well told and interesting as any of Fogazzaro's other novels. His customary skill in depicting the background and in portraying the characters' emotions and relationships is very much in evidence. In contrast with the two preceding stories of the tetralogy, however, there is relatively little humor or satirical genre-portrayal. Music plays a small part, and exists only as background in one or two passages. There is almost no use of dialect; only a few phrases in Roman dialect occur in the final episodes. Unfortunately, the intellectual content of *Il santo* and debates over its validity have largely obscured the novel's great literary merits.

After *Il santo* was published, there were some fears that it might provoke the wrath of the ecclesiastical authorities because it contained much stronger and more direct criticism than even *Piccolo mondo moderno*. Pius X had a personal dislike for Fogazzaro and his works; nevertheless, some of Fogazzaro's friends who were supposedly in a position to know assured him that no trouble would arise.[19] It was therefore quite unexpected when *Il santo* was placed on the Index on April 4, 1906. This event was, naturally, a great shock for Fogazzaro. At first, he indicated that he would submit unconditionally to the official condemnation and would thenceforth remain silent. His silence did not last long. In the following years he continued to give lectures and write essays expounding his ideas, and to take part in the activities of the "reformist" group.[20] Fogazzaro was invited to give a lecture at the École des Hautes Études ("School of Advanced Studies") in Paris, on "The Ideas of Giovanni Selva." This was delivered on January 18, 1907, and repeated at Geneva soon thereafter. Despite his efforts to remain within the limits of orthodoxy, he was accused by his detractors of "Protestant-

izing." His definitive statement of faith was given in a short essay
La parola di *Don Giuseppe Flores* ("The Word of Don Giuseppe
Flores"), which was not published until after Fogazzaro's death.[21]

III   Leila

A number of younger persons had come to look on Fogazzaro as a
leader, and on themselves as his disciples. One of the earliest of
these was a priest, Don Sebastiano Rumor (1862 - 1928), who wrote
the first biography of Fogazzaro while the latter was still living, and
published it in 1895.[22] Another was Tommaso Gallarati-Scotti
(1878 - 1966) who became Fogazzaro's favorite confidant in the
final years. Fogazzaro continued to attract epistolary correspondence from young women who were enthusiastic over his novels
and his ideas on religion. With one of these, a Swiss Italian from
Lugano (very near Oria) named Agnese Blank, he had an extensive
exchange of letters from 1908 onwards. He succeeded for a time in
persuading her to his point of view, and converting her from a skeptic into a believing Catholic. However, she later lost her faith again,
unlike Felicitas Buchner who had remained a devout Catholic, oc-
cupying herself with religiously oriented works of charity (to which
Fogazzaro contributed generously with both time and money).

Fogazzaro's pattern of life remained, in his sixties, as active and
varied as previously. He had a new villa, "La Montanina," built
between 1906 and 1908 near Velo d'Àstico, and made it his home
base. He, his wife, and his daughter Maria travelled extensively in
northern and central Italy, dividing their time between "La Montanina," his belovèd Valsolda, and Rome. His literary activities continued, with the production of some new poetry and with work on
the final novel of the Maironi tetralogy, *Leila*. Begun in 1909, it was
finished in May, 1910, and published on November 12 of the same
year.

As the story of *Leila* opens, an old man, Marcello Trento, and his
adopted daughter, Lelia Camin, are living at "La Montanina," near
Velo d'Àstico. Her parents are separated, and both are of dubious
character. Her father Giròlamo ("Momi") is a scheming, dissolute
wastrel, and her mother is a lady of doubtful virtue. Marcello's son
Andrea, a disciple of Benedetto-Piero (Maironi), had been engaged
to Lelia. After a disagreement, Andrea had given her a ring with the
name *Leila*, which she had planned to take on marrying him. After
Andrea's untimely death, Marcello has taken Lelia into his home

out of love for her. He knows that he will not live much longer and wants to make her his sole heir; but she is opposed to this plan. Marcello, just before the story opens, has invited Andrea's closest friend, Màssimo Alberti, a young doctor, to "La Montanina," in the hope that Lelia will fall in love with him and marry him. She, however, suspects Màssimo of being a vulgar fortune-hunter, and is quite cold towards him.

Near "La Montanina," in the Villino delle Rose ("Little Villa of the Roses"), lives an old lady, Donna Fedele Vayla di Brea, a former flame of Marcello's and a close friend ever since the death of his wife. She and the gentle, kindly local priest, Don Aurelio, have given shelter and care to an itinerant Protestant colporteur of Bibles, Pestagran, who had been badly beaten up by the ignorant peasants of a neighboring village. Pestagran was converted to Protestantism on a trip to England. Reactionary enemies of Don Aurelio within the church engage in maneuvers against him, so that, for having befriended Pestagran, he is ordered to leave his parish. He discourages his parishioners from protesting and departs.

Màssimo falls in love with Lelia, as Marcello had hoped. Seeing his love unrequited, however, he leaves for Milan, where he sees an advertisement of a vacancy for the post of *mèdico condotto* (village doctor) at Dasio, a remote village in the Valsolda above Oria. He goes there and obtains the position. Marcello dies, leaving all his property to Lelia. As she is still a minor, "Momi" Camin has the legal right to act on her "behalf"; he descends on "La Montanina" with his disreputable cronies. Lelia is in such despair that she attempts suicide. She does not succeed because Pestagran has seen her behaving strangely and informs Donna Fedele who arrives in time to save Lelia. The latter moves out of "La Montanina," leaving it in her father's control, and stays at the Villino delle Rose with Donna Fedele.

Through reading a letter which Màssimo has written to Donna Fedele, Leila becomes convinced that he does indeed love her. She feels an unconquerable desire to go and join him. Both of them have been rather skeptical in their views of religion, but they begin to feel drawn to Benedetto's approach to Christianity. By a trick, Lelia gets away from her father, and makes her way to Milan and Oria, where she rejoins Màssimo. They declare their mutual love; she is now willing to change her name to Leila, as a sign of her readiness to marry him.

Donna Fedele has been concealing from every-one the fact that she is fatally ill. Her condition becomes so bad, however, that she sets out for Turin to see a specialist, although it is probably too late. At Milan, she changes direction and proceeds to Porto Ceresio,[23] and thence by boat to Oria.

In the meanwhile, plans have been made to observe Benedetto's last wish, which was to have his mortal remains transferred to Oria, to the cemetery there beside the graves of his parents Franco and Luisa and his wife Elisa. Don Aurelio has come from Milan (where he has gone after leaving his parish) and he, Màssimo, and about a hundred villagers charter a boat and go down to Porto Ceresio to meet the train bringing the coffin from Rome. It arrives after some delay, due to official obstructionism. At Porto Ceresio, the group is joined by a veiled foreign lady and her maid who go to Oria on the boat carrying Benedetto's coffin, but stay on the edge of the proceedings. The company sing the De Profundis on the way back. After a brief ceremony, in which Don Aurelio eulogizes Benedetto and his earthly mission, the coffin is interred. Jeanne slips away, never to be heard from again. Màssimo and Leila will remain in Dasio, devoting themselves to the humble task of caring for the health of the villagers. Donna Fedele, after atrocious sufferings, dies serenely the next day.

Some have suggested that, since the novel deals with a number of other characters besides Lelia Camin, and since almost all through the story she is referred to as Lelia, it should not have been named Leila. She is, nevertheless, the main personage of the tale, and it deals with the development of her character, from her being "Lelia" to her becoming "Leila". At the outset, she is rather negative, not in her intelligence or artistic ability (she is a good pianist), but in her attitude toward life. Although willing to live in Marcello's household and be treated as his daughter, she does not go towards him, psychologically, far enough to accept the heritage which he wishes to leave her. Significantly, she lets him use the tu of familiarity to her, but uses only the Lei of formal direct address back to Marcello. As a result of previous experiences, she is suspicious of Màssimo's motives. It takes Donna Fedele's intervention to persuade Lelia of his sincerity and love. It is only after her unsuccessful attempt at suicide and rescue by Pestagran and Donna Fedele that she realizes her love for Màssimo and begins to assume a more positive attitude toward life. The rest of the story deals with her development to the point where, overcoming her waywardness of temperament, she is willing to be at one with Màssimo and thenceforth be "Leila". Some of her characteristics, especially her appearance and mannerisms, were drawn from Agnese Blank, but, as Fogazzaro wrote Agnese,[24] Lelia resembled her only in part. Fogazzaro's first impulse to write *Leila* came after the death of his wife's cousin Angelina Mangilli Lampertico, with the idea of enshrining her in a story as he had done for Felicitas Buchner in *Il mistero del poeta* and for his father in *Piccolo mondo antico*. She was the model for Donna Fedele in the story—*la Dama bianca delle rose* "the white lady of the roses," as Pestagran calls her. In Donna Fedele, Fogazzaro portrayed what he considered the permanently attractive features of feminine character, regardless of age. Her religion, especially, is the embodiment of charity and kindness, extending even to being a good Samaritan to an anti-Catholic like Pestagran. He responds in like manner to her, telling her that he will not try to convert her to Protestantism because she is "a truly Christian Catholic." Donna Fedele has an old cousin, Eufemia, her companion, who plays no major rôle in the development of the story, but who is somewhat comic and at the same time touching in her naïve simplicity, religiosity, and loving care for Fedele in the latter's terminal illness.

Of the masculine characters, Màssimo is said to have been drawn from Tommaso Gallarati-Scotti, the author's last and most beloved follower. Marcello Trento is both Fogazzaro's father and Fogazzaro himself, complete with the love of music and flowers which they both shared. Don Aurelio is another of Fogazzaro's idealized priests, of the same kind as Don Innocenzo in *Malombra* and Don Giuseppe Flores in *Piccolo mondo moderno*. The two other priests, more advanced in the ecclesiastical hierarchy, who intrigue against Don Aurelio and succeed in having him banished from his parish, are satirical portraits of the type of Pharisaical hypocrites whom Fogazzaro blamed for the evils of modern Catholicism.

In *Leila*, Fogazzaro abandoned his earlier practice of giving fictitious names to well-known houses, localities, or geographical features like streams, lakes, or mountains. His own house ("La Montanina") and all the surrounding countryside are described in detail and with their own names, so that it is possible to follow the comings and goings of the characters on a map of the region. The former steam-tram from Arsiero to Thiene, the stations from Vicenza to Milan and Porto Ceresio, the journey by boat thence to Oria, the Hotel Terminus in Milan,[25] are all presented as they were at the time *Leila* was written in 1909.

Beyond the origins of the characters in *Leila*, we must consider the message of the story, in relation to Fogazzaro's own situation at the end of his life and that of those who shared his outlook on the world and on the Catholic religion. After the encyclical *Pascendi* in 1907, there was a grave problem facing those who, like Fogazzaro, accepted the decision as final and stayed within the Roman church: what could be done about picking up the pieces and carrying on? His answer is clearly given in *Leila*: to accept the official decision (no matter how self-serving and objectionable the ecclesiastical hierarchy might be), and to devote oneself to the service of humanity, in no matter how obscure a position and for no matter how little reward—in short, *bene vixit qui bene latuit* ("he has lived well who has remained well out of sight"). The lesson of *Leila* is largely addressed to the younger generation, that of Màssimo and Lelia. The older generation—represented by Marcello Trento, Don Giuseppe Flores, Don Aurelio, and Donna Fedele—have been defeated in their spiritual aims, fully as much as Verga's *I vinti* ("The Conquered") are in their material goals. Their best hopes, symbolized by Benedetto in religion and by Marcello's son Andrea in personal relationships, have been destroyed by authority or by fate, and they themselves are, by the beginning of *Leila*, dead or dying.

Lelia's relation to Màssimo and that of both of them to Marcello is highly significant. Their initial function is that of surrogates. At the beginning of *Leila*, Lelia is living in Marcello's household as a replacement for his dead son Andrea. Marcello looks on Lelia as his daughter-in-law that might have been, and hopes that she will eventually marry Màssimo and thus make the latter into an effective son-substitute for Marcello. The dead Andrea had represented his father's best hopes for the future in every-day life, just as Benedetto had represented those of his followers for religious reform. Màssimo and Lelia represent a substitute for those hopes, as well as for the real person Andrea.

Lelia's origin is also significant. She has come into the tetralogy from outside, with no connection with any-one in the Maironi family or others in the story. Her ancestry is dubious—a phenomenon which always, in Fogazzaro's novels, has cultural-symbolic overtones, as in the instance of Daniele Cortis' harridan of a mother and in that of Violet Yves' unnamed first lover in *Il mistero del poeta*. She has already rejected her immoral mother, and her dishonest father and his shady cronies, before the story begins. At the end of the novel, she abandons her inheritance, even that which she has received under Marcello's will, to her dissolute father. Like Piero Maironi, she finally reaches the stage of giving up all her previous associations and heritage to devote herself to other concerns which Fogazzaro clearly wishes us to view as higher, although less lucrative.

Lelia is like Luisa Maironi, as many readers have noticed, in several ways: she is intellectual, rationalistic, sensitive, and proud. In religious matters, she is skeptical, willing at the most to accept a generalized and rather Unitarian (if not, indeed, rather pantheistic) belief in an omnipresent Deity. When she finally perceives her love for Màssimo and yields to it, she is willing to accept his beliefs, but only because of personal affection. Like Luisa, also, Lelia can be interpreted, in symbolic terms, as representing an aspect of Italian cultural life: in Lelia's case, that part of the Italian intellectual and cultural heritage which had its origins in questionable honesty and morality—from the immoralism of medieval *novellistica* down through the cynicism of, say, Machiavelli's *Mandràgola* ("The Mandrake"), to the bohemianism of the *Scapigliatura milanese*, which Fogazzaro knew well. Her decision to join Màssimo represents Fogazzaro's hope that Italian intellectuals might reject this (not inconsiderable) side of their cultural heritage and come over to the side of the unassuming, self-sacrificing altruism symbolized by Màssimo.

Màssimo Alberti's profession as a doctor is important. If Benedetto and his followers are not to be granted their hopes, to help and to improve the efficacy of the church's work in ameliorating mankind's spiritual condition, those who come afterwards are to renounce this aim and devote themselves to serving man's physical needs. At the end of *Leila*, Màssimo expects to accomplish this aim by becoming the *mèdico condotto* of Dasio, about as far out of contact with the world as is possible physically and bureaucratically, and at the very humblest level of the public health organization.

Pestagran, the Protestant colporteur of Bibles, is also a significant figure in the symbolism of *Leila*. He is literally "despised and rejected of men," and Don Aurelio and Donna Fedele are the only ones to show him true Christian love, after he has been badly beaten by the local people. His function in the story, aside from exemplifying this characteristic of Donna Fedele and Don Aurelio, is to represent Fogazzaro's attitude towards Protestantism as practised by Italian converts. (No mention is made anywhere in Fogazzaro's works, that I have been able to find, of the indigenous, pre-

Lutheran Italian Protestants, the Waldensians.) Fogazzaro seems to be telling us, through the example of Pestagran, that Protestantism can only be something imported from outside, and that it is doomed to incomprehension and rejection by virtually all. Donna Fedele and Don Aurelio give him Christian love and charity, but of course are not interested in the doctrines which he wishes to spread. The rest of his compatriots are too sunk in superstition and dominated by the ecclesiastical powers-that-be to do anything but revile and maltreat him. Nevertheless, it is Pestagran who alerts Donna Fedele to the danger of Leila's drowning herself. This episode, too, is symbolic, telling us that Italian intellectual life will be saved from destroying itself only by pure Christianity, freed from all sectarianism or dogmatism.

Although Benedetto dies at the end of *Il santo*, his spirit is present in the background of *Leila* all the way through the story, in the memory of its principal characters and as an inspiration to them. The next-to-the-last episode of *Leila* involves Benedetto's re-burial in Valsolda. Jeanne Dessalle appears briefly, without taking an active part in the ceremony, only to disappear immediately afterwards. Obviously the re-burial of Benedetto symbolizes Fogazzaro's abandonment of all hope for inner regeneration of the Roman church from non-ecclesiastical sources, and Jeanne's disappearance symbolizes abandonment of non-Italian cultural attractions. But why are Benedetto's remains transferred to Valsolda, instead of being left in Rome? Inasmuch as Valsolda always represented for Fogazzaro, from the earliest times of his life, his personal inner quite and peace, the re-burial clearly signifies that these former hopes are to be entirely disassociated from Rome (i.e., from the visible church) and to remain henceforth inactive and be remembered only in Fogazzaro's own heart.

The Maironi tetralogy affords, in its content, a résumé of Fogazzaro's outlook on modern Italian life and culture. In its official fate, it indicates the dilemma in which he found himself. He was too desirous of reform to accept prevalent ecclesiastical attitudes and behavior; but, when the chips were down, he was too firm a believer in ultimate ecclesiastical authority to reject it in favor of reform. One might even say that the Maironi tetralogy is, taken as a whole, the symbolic biography of the dilemma of Fogazzaro and many of his forward-looking contemporaries. The last word on the matter is given to Don Aurelio in his brief allocution over Benedetto's coffin in the final chapter of *Leila:*

Listen. This man has spoken a great deal about religion, faith, and works. He was not a Pontiff making authoritative *ex cathedra* pronouncements; he was not a prophet; he may, in speaking a great deal, have erred a great deal; he may have expressed propositions and concepts which the authority of the church would be right in rejecting. The true character of his activity did not lie in discussing theological questions in which he might have been in error; it was the determination of the religious worth of this spirit incarnated in the life, the feelings, and the works of men. He always proclaimed his faithful obedience to the authority of the Church, to the Holy See of the Roman Pontiff. [. . .]

He died trusting that, once the evil spirits with which the Church is afflicted have been cast back, one day, within the gates of Hell, all men who have received baptism and invoke the name of Christ would be united in a single religious people around the Holy See of the Roman Pontiff. He begs his friends to pray for this great purpose.

These sentiments, attributed to Benedetto in Don Aurelio's speech, are clearly Fogazzaro's own, reflecting his feeling, on the one hand, of submission to the authority which had rejected his heart-felt wishes, and, on the other hand, of hope that those wishes might some day, nevertheless, be granted.

As a novel, *Leila* represents, to a considerable extent, a return to the manner of *Piccolo mondo antico*. It is primarily a novel of character, and only to a much less degree a novel of ideas. Intellectual and religious concerns are by no means absent, but—with the exception of Don Aurelio's final allocution just quoted—they are not set forth in theoretical discussions, but are embodied in persons and their relationships (for instance, Marcello and Lelia, Lelia and Màssimo, or Donna Fedele and Pestagran). The characters, especially Lelia and Donna Fedele, are memorable, and their vicissitudes are narrated in a realistic yet lyrical vein. *Leila* was Fogazzaro's swan-song, and a worthy one.

IV   *The End*

Two weeks after the publication of *Leila*, Fogazzaro fell ill with a calculous condition of the liver, and never recovered. After an unsuccessful operation on March 4, 1911, he lingered for three days, and died on March 7. His passing was treated almost as a national loss, accompanied by extensive publicity and messages of condolence.

The ecclesiastical authorities were unable to perceive the obvious symbolism of *Leila,* indicating Fogazzaro's abandonment of his hopes for reform from within the Catholic church, and his advice to the younger generation to devote themselves to humble service to humanity. The anticlerical satire of a few chapters and the evocation of Benedetto's ideals were clearly too much for the Vatican to countenance. *Leila* was placed on the Index on May 8, 1911, two months and a day after Fogazzaro's death.

CHAPTER 7

Subject-Matter and
Narrative Technique

I *Personality-Factors*

F OGAZZARO'S chief concern, in virtually all his writings, was with human beings and their relationships with each other, as individuals and (somewhat less) as members of society and the church. His novels deal, therefore, primarily with character and to a lesser extent with manners, insofar as the latter reveal character. Ideas, ideals, and abstract theories are also present to a certain extent, but are important only insofar as they affect the lives of his personages. Even *Il Santo* is not an exception to this statement, since Benedetto's ideals and theoretical proclamations are closely intertwined with his own personal history.

In general, Fogazzaro's chief characters are drawn from the strata of society with which he was best acquainted, the lower-upper and upper-middle classes of northern Italy. His normal procedure was to take as his models people whom he knew well and then to add further characteristics and imagine them in various situations. People of all social classes occur, however, in great number, as secondary and minor figures, especially from *Daniele Cortis* onwards. Fogazzaro portrays them with sympathy and understanding, even when they play only a very small part in the development of the action. The lower classes are by no means absent. Some of Fogazzaro's most likeable characters are of the servant or peasant class, such as the page-boy Rico in *Malombra* or the colporteur Pestagran in *Leila*.

The clergy occupy a special place in Fogazzaro's novels and short stories, since he knew them so well and introduced them so frequently. They, too, are of all types, including the simple-minded and gullible Don Rocco of *Pereat Rochus*. Regardless of social origin, his preferred type of cleric is of course the saintly, non-dogmatic priest, from Don Innocenzo in *Malombra* to Don Giuseppe Flores in *Piccolo mondo moderno* and Don Aurelio in *Leila*. These priests are all too likely, in Fogazzaro's stories as in real life, to be pushed aside and victimized by not so admirable ecclesiastics who are less intent on living up to Christian precepts than they are on preserving vested interests, whether in established dogma or their own advancement.

Fogazzaro's heroes and heroines are psychologically complex, just as he himself was. They cannot be summed up in simple formulas, such as that they are all *affettivi puri* "purely emotional types".[1] Of course emotion plays a major rôle in their psychological make-up and in their relations to each other, as it does in all normal people's lives. Each of his major personages has, however, one or more other characteristics which, in combination with their emotions, produce various reactions.

As in most of our European and American fiction, love between man and woman occupies the first place in all of Fogazzaro's novels and most of his short stories. In none of them, though, does the course of true love run smoothly, because it is always interfered with by conflicting factors within the psyches of one or both lovers. Because of the former popularity of *Daniele Cortis*, and the great impression that the conflict between love and duty in the hearts of Daniele and Elena made on its readers, this conflict has often been thought to be the principal or only theme in Fogazzaro's treatment of love. Yet, if we look at his other heroes and heroines, we find many other types of conflict, all of them internal. Singleness of purpose characterizes only the unnamed narrator of *Il mistero del poeta;* in his case, it is an external phenomenon, the reappearance of Violet's earlier lover and her sudden death, that takes her from him. In several instances, two loves or two types of love are in conflict within the same person, for instance in Silla's sensual love for Marina and more spiritualized love for Edith; Edith's love for Silla, unavowed because of her devotion to her father; or Piero's love for Jeanne, which is surpassed by his love for Christ's gospel.

In other cases, the development of the character's love is hindered by some other kind of factor. Violet Yves refuses for a long time to yield to her Italian suitor's insistence, both because she is engaged to Toplerus junior and because she feels shame on account of her earlier love-affair. Lelia Camin is too intellectually proud and too suspicious of Màssimo Alberti's motives to believe in his sincerity, and at the same time she is ashamed of her unsavory parents. When she does avow her love to Màssimo, she feels so humble that she cannot bring herself to use the familiar *tu* to him, but persists in using the formal mode of address with *Ella* and *Lei* in both her conversation and her love-letters. The crucial example of this type of interference from non-amorous factors is the split in Franco and Luisa Maironi's originally happy marriage, caused by the divergence in their views of what constitutes justice and what should be done about the old Marchesa's having robbed them of Franco's inheritance. In each of these instances, the psychological trauma is so great as to cause doubt, hesitation, and anguish, just as it does in so many cases in real life—beginning, of course, with Fogazzaro's own intense inner experience. Of all the major love-affairs in Fogazzaro's novels, the only one to have the traditional "happy ending" is that of Màssimo and Lelia, and it comes about only after much travail on their part.[2]

Yet it must not be thought that Fogazzaro was concerned exclusively with unhappy or star-crossed love. Professor Gilardoni's successful courtship of Ester Bianchi, which Fogazzaro narrates with mixed tenderness and amusement, forms a counter-balance to the marital difficulties of Franco and Luisa. In *Un'idea di Ermes Torranza*, Bianca and her estranged husband, both of whom wish deep in their hearts for a reconciliation, are brought together again by Torranza's posthumous mediation at the end of the story. Maestro Chieco's "fiasco" consists in his unintentionally bringing together his friend and the latter's innamorata after their separation. Fogazzaro's vision was broad enough to include all kinds of love-relationships, even though, in his major works, the serious view prevails.

Fogazzaro's basic seriousness extends well beyond the love-emotion, reaching to his own and many of his characters' ultra-terrestrial aspirations. Some of his personages are not concerned, one way or the other, with their relationships to God, to the Christian religion, or the hereafter. Of this type are Marina in *Malombra* and Violet Yves in *Il mistero del poeta*: nominally Catholics, they make little mention of their religion nor does it enter to any extent into the determination of their actions. Others, especially Luisa Maironi and Lelia Camin, are too strongly intellectual and have too much faith in their own mental abilities to be inclined towards mysticism or an emotional approach to matters of the spirit. When such characters' psychological strength is undermined, as is Luisa's after the death of Ombretta, or when their minds become deranged, as does Marina's, they tend to take refuge in pseudo-spiritualistic beliefs and occultist practices. The Christian gospel, as embodied (though not always actualized) in the Roman Catholic church, is clearly what Fogazzaro regarded and intended his readers to regard as the one truly satisfactory approach to religion. Yet this approach, if made the basis of one's behavior—action in the cases of Daniele Cortis and Piero-Benedetto, inaction in the case of Franco Maironi—brings its adherents into difficulties because it clashes so strongly with the realities of the ecclesiastical, political, and social world. The conflicts thus engendered are one of the major sources of tension and hence of drama in Fogazzaro's novels. The only solution he seems to suggest for them, when all is said and done, is to act as Màssimo and Leila plan to do, going to places and positions far out of the lime-light and doing good for humanity insofar as is possible, without further questioning or opposition to authority.

Fogazzaro's characters are not static in their psychological make-up. They change and develop as experience teaches them, particularly with respect to their religious and moral obligations. Most of his major characters are stronger at the end of the story than they are at the beginning because they have suffered and learned. Corrado Silla is the main exception to this generalization. He has come to consider himself *inetto a vivere* "unfit to live," and does not learn from his experiences with Marina and Edith. His inability to overcome the fascination which Marina exercises over him is the cause of his willingness to return to the Ormengo palace and hence of his ultimate death. Fogazzaro's later heroes and heroines may go through periods of discouragement and apparent failure, but they are in the end victorious over their difficulties. This pattern is true even of Benedetto at the end of *Il santo*. Although his physique gives way under his sufferings, he has accomplished his mission, both to spread Christ's gospel in so far as lies within his power, and, on the personal level, to bring Jeanne back to the faith.

Other emotions besides love and religious feeling can play a major rôle in the psychology of some of Fogazzaro's characters—as do, for instance, deluded credulity in Don Rocco of *Pereat Rochus,* bitter disappointment in Vasco of *Eden Anto,* or repentance for past disobedience in the eponymous heroine of the short story *Fedele.* His older personages have usually attained an inner serenity through their earlier sufferings, so that they often show kindness and love, giving generous assistance to the members of the younger generation, as do Elena's uncle Lao for her and her husband, Luisa's uncle Piero for her and Franco, and Marcello Trento and Donna Fedele Vayla di Brea for Màssimo and Leila. Fogazzaro's lesser characters are not normally studied in depth. They appear (as in real life) with all kinds of traits, which manifest themselves as they affect the lives of the major personages. Virtually every minor character, however, is given some individuality, with features of appearance or behavior described in considerable detail. One instance must suffice for a great many. In *Leila*, when Lelia takes the train for Milan to go to Valsolda, she has as compartment-mates four other people:

> In that compartment were travelling four other persons, an old lady with a young lady about thirty years old, a young commercial traveller, and a kind of vulgarly elegant café-singer. [. . . .] The young lady betrayed, talking with the young man, a rare effervescence of amorous temperament. She paraded her culture of novels and plays, and, since the young man had spoken of a forthcoming trip to Egypt, she tried to get him to promise her a scarab. The young man would have been happier, it was altogether too obvious, to promise scarabs to the café-singer, but she, however, paid no attention to his sideways glances and instead kept looking a great deal at Lelia.

These travelling-companions are important in the story only as they impinge briefly on Lelia's existence. The commercial traveller ultimately, after the others have left the train, molests her and forces her to move to another compartment, and makes her feel all the more that she belongs to Màssimo and to him only. These minor characters and the small events connected with them remain in the reader's memory, however, as they would have remained in Lelia's as part of the experience during the train-trip.

Certain types of emotion and behavior are notable for their absence from Fogazzaro's stories. Hard-heartedness is not uncommon. Sometimes it comes from greed, as in the case of Vasco's creditor Marcòn in *Eden Anto*. In other instances, it is due to narrow-mindedness, as in many of the bigoted, reactionary clerics and their lay partisans, whose prototypes Fogazzaro knew so well. Downright hatred, on the other hand, is found only in Marina di Malombra, and in her case it is due to insanity. Many people die, but death is regarded in general as a prelude to a life to come, so that Fogazzaro tends to underplay its less spiritually inspiring aspects.[3] Deliberate murder occurs only twice, again in *Malombra*, when Marina causes the death of Césare d'Ormengo by frightening him, and later shoots Silla. Violence of any kind is rare, particularly in direct description, as is also vulgarity in actions or speech. Homosexuality is naturally completely absent. In general, Fogazzaro's characters manifest the behavior-patterns of North Italian gentlefolk, the kind of society which he frequented and knew best, and hence described.

The predominant tenor of life in Fogazzaro's stories is quiet, with his characters leading a fairly regular day-to-day existence in their homes, whether large or small. Their favorite occupations include reading, playing cards or other games (such as the billiards in the opening chapter of *Daniele Cortis*, accompanied by extensive discussion of lawn-tennis), and making music when they are indoors. Out of doors, they cultivate their flowers and gardens, and walk (less often ride) in the country. Naturally, not all Fogazzaro's characters belong to the leisure class, and he describes many of them as they go about their daily business. In the course of all these activities, they think, reflect, and feel extensively, and of course converse with each other. Their crises normally come slowly, taking time to mature as one or another cause of conflict gradually looms larger. When the main crisis of each story finally erupts, it does so relatively quietly, with violence only (as just mentioned) in the two murders committed by Marina. In other instances, there are strong feelings, tears, and sobs, normally accompanied by intense but polite speech. Exceptionally, the Baron of Santa Giulia, in *Daniele Cortis*, uses vulgar expressions when he is forced to submit to his rescuers' conditions in order to escape from his debts; this is a sign of his baseness. These conditions are especially favorable for the type of personality which Fogazzaro studied in the greatest detail: sensitive, reflective, self-analysing, often (by no means always) unsure of itself and slow to come to a decision, but (a fact which many of Fogazzaro's critics have failed to notice) firm once the decision is reached.

II *Human Relationships*

Fogazzaro's characters live, suffer, and die, not only as individuals, but in groupings, and in relation to each other and to God. The family is the most obvious of these groupings, and it is present, for both good and evil, in all of his novels. Some of his couples are happy in the marital state, for instance Count Lao and

Countess Tarquinia in *Daniele Cortis*, the old Marchese and Marchesa Scremin in *Piccolo mondo moderno*, or—although (perhaps because!) theirs is a *mariage blanc*—Giovanni and Maria Selva in *Il santo*. Màssimo and Leila expect to form a happy marriage at the end of *Leila*. Some of Fogazzaro's widows or widowers keep their deceased spouses and their married love alive in their memory, as do especially the narrator of *Il mistero del poeta* and Marcello Trento. Marriage has brought less than complete happiness, often great unhappiness, to a number of other couples. We need only think of Èlena and the Baron of Santa Giulia, of Franco and Luisa Maironi, of Piero and Elisa Maironi, and (among the lesser characters) the *bargnìf* Pasotti and his deaf, abused, but uncomplaining old wife Barborìn.

The relationship between the generations can also be either friendly and loving, or strained, even to the breaking-point, as between Franco and his grandmother. For the most part, parents and children, or uncles and their nephews and nieces, love and cherish each other. Edith and her long-lost father Steinegge set the pattern for the parent-child relationship. The best-remembered example of avuncular affection is that of Piero Ribera for his grand-niece Ombretta. In the latter, Fogazzaro has created one of the few truly memorable child characters in all of Italian literature, both in her own right and for her relation to her parents and uncle.

Much more common in every-day life, and in Fogazzaro's novels, than in most other fiction is the friendship between priest and layman (whether the latter is a parishioner or not) beyond the confines of the confessional. We have already mentioned the various noble priests who keep recurring in Fogazzaro's stories, and the inspiration which they afford their friends. Not all the latter are, necessarily, even believers, for instance Edith Steinegge's father Andreas. He, as well as his daughter and Silla, is strongly impressed by the loving kindness of Don Innocenzo. Not only their relation to individual priests, but their membership in the Roman church is felt by a number of Fogazzaro's personages—especially, of course, Piero Maironi—to be a central concern of their lives, no matter how its hierarchy may behave.

III   *The Background*

Few novelists have been as attentive as Fogazzaro to the environment, natural and architectural, in which the activities of his

characters take place. At the same time, he was especially intent on
perceiving and conveying to the reader the life that he felt in
everything. As Piero Giacosa said of him,[4] "In every thing, animate
or inanimate, he sought and infused life." As early as "Il Libro
d'Enrico" ("The Book of Enrico") in *Miranda*, Fogazzaro has the
young poet, when he returns to the country-side and nature after
being disgusted with the "civilized" world, say:

> Susurrava la selva e agitava
> Le verdi chiome redivive appena,
> A me d'intorno, sul pendìo del monte;
> Ivan tra l'erba folta rivi lìmpidi,
> Spumeggiavano al sol le cascatelle,
> Gorgheggiavan dall'alto i capineri.
> Ero solo: nè Driadi nè Amadriadi
> Stavan meco ad ascoltar; ma certo
> I capineri, l'acque, la foresta
> Parlavan tutti insieme a qualche amico
> Spìrito, e ciaschedun parea volesse
> Vincer di voce tènera i compagni.
> Arsi allor di confondervi la mia,
> In piè levarmi e dir versi soavi
> Più che il gaio ciarlar d'acque, d'augelli;
> Versi soavi ch'anima vivente
> Non udrebbe giammai.

"The forest was whispering and was tossing its green tresses, which
had just returned to live, around me, on the mountain-slope; clear
brooks were flowing through the thick grass, the little water-falls
were foaming in the sun-shine, and the blackbirds were warbling on
high. I was alone; no Dryads or Hamadryads were with me to listen;
but certainly the blackbirds, the waters, the forest were speaking
together to some friendly spirit, and each one seemed to wish to
out-do its companions in tender expression. Then I dared to mingle
my voice with theirs, to rise to my feet and to speak verses softer
than the cheerful babble of waters and birds—soft verses which no
living soul would ever hear!"

Fogazzaro was a great flower-lover; we are told[5] that when he
arrived at his house in Oria, his first concern would always be to go
around and look at all the flowers to find how they had been faring.
He knew the names of the various genera and species, and introduced them extensively into both his poetry and his prose. They

often serve as symbols, for instance the American aloe (*agave americana*), which came to represent for him the late flowering of a lofty and pure love.[6] This flower and its symbolism keep recurring, from the poem *L'agave americana in Valsolda*, to *Il mistero del poeta* and even later, in connection with Felicitas Buchner, in his diary (up to 1894). Trees also have, as it were, personalities of their own, and can be the objects of human affection. On occasion, Fogazzaro speaks of plants and trees as if they had a share in human activities and affections. In *Un'idea di Ermes Torranza*, Bianca persuades her un-poetic, avaricious father to spare "the beloved poplars which had so often seen her run and jump, before [she went off to] school, with her rustic friends." After she has broken with her husband and returned to her home at Monte San Doná: "She had indeed believed, at first, that they [the poplars] looked sternly at her; but then she told them so many things that all coolness between her and the old trees disappeared. Two months after her return, when she saw, one bright November day, that the last hoarfrosts and the strong wind of the previous day had stripped them of leaves almost to their tops, those quivering yellowish-reddish crests gave her an inexpressible melancholy; she felt that the poplars were greeting her from afar like faithful friends, near to dying, to losing their speech and their senses."

Fauna, on the other hand, as opposed to flora, play very little part in Fogazzaro's stories. His characters do not, in general, have pets, nor are they emotionally involved with animals as they are with plants and trees. When animals are introduced, they are often portrayed humorously or contemptuously.

The setting of a story—including the landscape and the objects which compose it, especially the houses—is of fundamental importance to Fogazzaro. Even when he seems to be describing the landscape for its own sake, he brings it into relation with human affairs, as in the often-cited description of the village of Castello in *Piccolo mondo antico*: "At Castello, the houses which press close together in a row on the tortuous brow of the mountain-side to enjoy the sun and the view of the lake for a long distance, all white and smiling towards that other unfortunate row of houses which stands sadly behind them, resemble certain fortunate people in the world who, in the presence of wretchedness which is too close, take a proud hostile stance, draw close together, and help each other to keep it back".

Fogazzaro correlated nature with his personages' actions and feelings in various ways. On occasion, features of nature are almost personified so that they seem to be looking at or saying things to the characters, as in Silla's second trip to the castle in *Malombra*. More often, things and their arrangements reflect people's ways of living and their psychology—the severity of the castle in relation to Count d'Ormengo in *Malombra*, the simplicity of Edith's and Steinegge's apartment in Milan in the same novel, or the fusty atmosphere of the old Marchesa Maironi's house in *Piccolo mondo antico*. The aspect of the landscape may change according to the state of mind of their person beholding it: after speaking with a "friend" of his mother's, Daniele Cortis feels that Lake Lugano and especially the mountain peaks look threatening, but when he thinks of Èlena the next morning he is calmer and it no longer seems menacing. In some instances, the landscape is described in considerable detail to help Fogazzaro emphasize the insensitivity of a character to its beauty or the person's preoccupation with inner concerns.

Not only sight, but also sound is involved in the characters' perception of the environment. The noise of the various water-courses—brooks, streams, water-falls—the singing of the birds, and even every-day noises like the rattle of carriage-wheels or the whistle of the steam-tram as it is heard from "La Montanina" or Donna Fedele's Villa of the Roses, play their part in arousing or reflecting personal emotions. Similarly, the sound of various persons' voices is presented as an essential part of the impression which they make. Fogazzaro's basic aim in describing the background as his characters perceive it through their senses (primarily sight and hearing, occasionally also smell) is to give the reader as full an understanding as possible of their total experience of reality.[7]

Much of the action of Fogazzaro's stories takes place indoors, rendering quite important the types of houses and furnishings which serve as settings.[8] In some instances—relatively few but quite striking—the main action centers around a large building, a *palazzo*,[9] of which the best example is that of Count Césare d'Ormengo in *Malombra*. In that novel, the size of the *palazzo*, and its many rooms and meanderings, are an essential aid to providing the half-mysterious atmosphere in which Marina's madness develops. Of less importance for the action of the story as a whole, but still highly functional in certain portions, are the *palazzi* of the Marchesa Orsola Maironi in *Piccolo mondo antico* and of the Scremin family in the following novel.

More frequent are large villas, which recur in several of the novels, for example Villa Carré and Villa Cortis in *Daniele Cortis*, Villa Diedo in *Piccolo mondo moderno*, or Villa Mayda (the Selvas' home) in *Il santo*. In the city, comparable settings are found in large town-houses or apartments, such as the salon of the Di Bella family in Milan which Silla visits, or the house of the Treuberg family in Eichstätt. These aristocratic or upper-bourgeois dwellings serve primarily as settings for large gatherings against which important personal encounters stand out in greater relief than they would otherwise. We need think only of the private conversations of Èlena and her uncle Lao or Daniele Cortis, of Jeanne and Piero at the musicale at Villa Diedo, or the meeting of the same couple after the gathering of "modernists" at the Selvas' villa in *Il santo*.

A more homely, intimate atmosphere is found in the smaller house or *villetta* of Fogazzaro's less pretentious personages, particularly Franco and Luisa's dwelling at Oria, and also "La Montanina" of Marcello Trento and Donna Fedele's *villino delle rose* in *Leila*. Nor are more humble types of lodging absent; in many episodes, Fogazzaro's characters either live in or visit modest, even poverty-stricken homes, hovels, or huts. Don Aurelio, in *Leila*, lives in an extremely simple parish-house, virtually Franciscan in its plainness, where he is able to live a chaste and intellectually active existence. Perhaps the most plebeian setting is found in the ultra-realistic short story *Il testamento dell'orbo di Rettòrgole* ("The Will of the Blind Man of Rettòrgole") in which the dying man has been moved, because of the filth and stench to which his terminal illness has given rise, to the hay-loft of the barn.

A relatively unusual type of setting for many episodes is found in churches. On occasion, a character will visit a church by himself, as do Enrico in *Miranda* and Silla in *Malombra*, or Piero in the chapel of the insane asylum in *Piccolo mondo moderno*. In other instances, a meeting takes place at or in a church, as when Edith Steinegge and her father are together with Don Innocenzo at the latter's church. Given Fogazzaro's intense interest in religious matters, it is not surprising that churches should be mentioned so often; but they are not necessarily always places of lofty inspiration. On entering Milan cathedral, Silla feels oppressed and downcast at first, only to be possessed later by amorous and very sensual thoughts of Marina.

Single rooms, as well, are closely related to the thoughts and actions of Fogazzaro's personages. The rooms may vary in size, from the reception-hall at Villa Diedo where Maestro Chieco and the other musicians give a concert, or the main living-room in "La

Montanina" where Marcello Trento and Lelia play the piano, to smaller, more intimate quarters. Of the latter, perhaps the most memorable are Èlena's study at Villa Carré and Marcello's at "La Montanina", where the most intimate moments of their inner lives are passed. Perhaps the most narrow, confining, and at the same time symbolic of spiritual concentration is the cave in which Piero-Benedetto lives at Jenne.

IV *Narrative Technique*

As De Rienzo has pointed out,[10] one of Fogazzaro's major innovations in the writing of novels in Italy was his presentation of his characters' experience of reality in depth, rather than in breadth. Almost all critics have taken the titles of two of his novels as their starting-point and have remarked that he leads his readers into a "little world," a microcosm in which life is observed and experienced intensely. In contrast to many other writers,[11] Fogazzaro limited his subject-matter and its locale strictly both to places and to personality-types which he himself had observed and stored in his memory. Almost all his stories are set in northern Italy, in an area extending from Turin on the west to Venice on the east, from the Dolomites on the north to Rome and the valley of the Aniene on the south. In *Il mistero del poeta*, the narrator travels to Germany, following very much the same itinerary that Fogazzaro himself took on his one trip to that country.

The period in which the action of the novels takes place is, likewise, wholly included in the span of Fogazzaro's own lifetime. For each one of his novels, precise dates can be established for the beginning and the end of the action.[12] He was old enough to remember, even though only as a child, the late Risorgimento, during which the action of *Piccolo mondo antico* takes place. All the other stories are set in Fogazzaro's mature years—in some instances, notably *Daniele Cortis*, *Piccolo mondo moderno*, and *Il santo*, too much so for many of his contemporaries who did not relish the open criticisms of his own times which formed an essential part of the stories.

To give his reader the feeling of having shared in the characters' experience, so that they remain in one's memory after one has finished the story, Fogazzaro uses several highly refined techniques. The most obvious of these is the selective but detailed description of the environments, and especially the individual features with which

the personages are most closely involved or which are somehow in-
dicative of their character. Here, for instance, is how one of Daniele
Cortis' political associates, Dr. Grigiolo, sees the main room in Villa
Cortis: "He entered the house. A colossal lamp was burning opposite the door on a table of unfinished wood, lighting up, from the
floor to the enormous black beams, the room with its four frowning
side doors, with its disorderly array of papers and books piled up in
confusion on the table, scattered over the sofa and the chairs, with
the two eagles placed with outspread wings in the corners opposite
the entrance. Between these two corners, the great door giving on
the garden was open."

The details of Cortis' living-room—the emphasis on the size of
the lamp, the beams, and the door, the lack of attention to elegance
and polish as manifested in the table and the confusion of books and
papers, the seriousness suggested by the "frowning" side doors and
the eagles—all give us an insight into the psychology of their owner
and set the stage for the colloquy between Dr. Grigiolo and Cortis,
in which the latter expounds his views on politics and religion.
Similar examples could be multiplied almost *ad infinitum* from all
of Fogazzaro's novels and short stories. Other memorable descriptions are those of Franco's study in his house in Oria, of the
Marchesa Orsola Maironi's living-room at Cressogno, and of "La
Montanina" at Velo d'Àstico.

Fogazzaro's descriptions cover not only the scenes but also the actions and thoughts of his characters. His technique was not that of
an ultra-realist, attempting to include in his description everything
that is to be observed in the external setting without relation to the
characters and their personalities, and at the same time renouncing
any effort to tell what is going on in the characters' minds.[13]
Throughout all his stories, Fogazzaro tells his personages' thoughts
and reactions to their experiences, again giving the reader the impression of having lived through and remembered the same events
and having had the same impressions.

When we meet some-one, we do not always perceive that person's basic qualities immediately. It often takes a certain length of
time and closeness of acquaintance to realize a given person's true
merits. Fogazzaro's method of narration takes this phenomenon into
account. In most of his stories, he introduces a character and lets the
reader observe him or her for some time, only gradually having the
personage reveal his or her true nature. The best-known instance of
this procedure is the way in which he first portrays the old

Marchesa Scremin in the first chapter of *Piccolo mondo moderno*, comically fussing over the whereabouts of an egg in Lent. Not until considerably farther on in the story do we realize, from her conversations with Piero and Don Giuseppe Flores, how noble a personality she has. This is by no means an isolated example, since a number of other personages, in this and other novels, are introduced in the same way.

The same procedure is evident in Fogazzaro's manner of beginning a story or a chapter of a novel. Instead of plunging *in medias res* or coming rapidly to the point of the narration, he usually begins with some minor (but, as it turns out later, significant) detail, and leads the reader gradually into the main stream of the story. The opening of *Un'idea di Ermes Torranza* is typical:

Profesor Farsatti of Padua, the same man who had with Monsieur Nisard the famous polemic over the *fabulaeque Manes* of Horace,[14] used to say of Monte San Donà 'What do you expect? French poetry!' The solitary palace, the old garden of the San Donà family were little less objectionable to him than 'monsiù Nisard', ever since the fall of 1846, when he had been invited there by its noble owners to eat thrushes, and starlings had gotten mixed in among them. From the avenue leading to the house, with its horse-chestnuts trimmed to the shape of cubes, to the maze, to the water-fountains, to the long stairway that leads up the hill; from the foundation to the heavy top floor of the palace, the good professor found everything pretentious and shabby, artificial and prosaic. 'What could you expect? French poetry!'

In the following paragraphs we learn that Professor Farsatti has died, sleeping on what Fogazzaro terms "his battle-field" of the Horatian verses *Nox fabulaeque Manes / Et domus exilis Plutonis* "Night and the storied spirits of the ancestors, and the narrow house of Pluto." The San Donà family, which was of French origin, has "come down in the world," and economies, already practised in 1846 (starlings mixed in with the thrushes at dinner), have become the mania of Bianca's father, the miserly Sior Beneto, for whom "neither French nor Italian poetry exists." He has allowed the place to go to rack and ruin; the only things saved, of those mentioned in the first paragraph, are the poplars, and those only at Bianca's insistence.

In the paragraph quoted, Professor Farsatti has nothing to do with the rest of the story, but he serves several purposes. He is typical of the former acquaintances of the family, who no longer visit Monte San Donà in its isolated location in the Euganean Hills. He justifies Fogazzaro's introduction—done gradually, in two steps—of the Horatian tag, which in its turn helps to establish an atmosphere of late autumnal decay and gloom. It also anticipates the final episode of the story, in which the old poet Torranza reunites Bianca and her husband even after he too has joined "the spirits of the ancestors and the narrow house of Pluto." Farsatti's comical anger over the starlings gives an initial indication of the declining fortunes of the San Donà family. The worthy professor's fussy polemic with a French classicist, and his reference to "French poetry," are characteristic of Italians' and especially Venetians' contempt for overly fancy and pretentious, empty Frenchified elegance. The whole situation affords us a picture of the narrow, constrained family-life in which Bianca has grown up.

On the other hand, Fogazzaro could be very brief in mentioning features which are essential to the outline of the plot, but omitting detail which would not add to the atmosphere or memorability of the story. After Bianca has married Emilio, she has in-law-trouble and leaves him: "Bianca had quite earnestly returned the love of the handsome blond young man who, after a long period of silent adoration, had come forward to ask her hand; but her parents-in-law—coarse, miserly, irritable— had proven intolerable to her. The husband, a kindly but weak man, had not dared to protect her as he ought; from this, anger and tears had resulted. There were no children; and so, Bianca had been able, in an out-burst of anger, to return to her lonely corner of the Euganean Hills, and to her venerable old poplars."

Fogazzaro's narrative art consists in knowing which features of a situation will both aid the reader's psychological penetration and remain in his memory as something vicariously but intensely experienced, and which will not.

Like Fogazzaro himself, many of his personages undertake relatively long trips. Fogazzaro's descriptions of these journeys correspond to the way in which we normally react to the scenery and background on our travels. We observe minute details which are well known to us, as long as we are in familiar territory; but, the less familiar the territory, the less we observe in the way of individual features and the more attention we pay to our fellow-travellers or to outstanding aspects of the landscape. When Donna Fedele sets out on her last journey, going to the station at Arsiero to take the train for Milan and Valsolda, she notices the church where she had taken communion two days previously, and sees "La Montanina." Once on the train from Arsiero, she closes her eyes so as not to see the details of the landscape. Franco Maironi, on leaving Oria, notices similarly the houses, the church, and all the other spots which were dear to him.[15] When Franco returns from Turin to Oria, Fogazzaro mentions at first only the major towns through which he passes. Then, as Franco comes closer to the border (crossing by a path normally used only by smugglers), the places mentioned become smaller and more frequent. Fogazzaro thus sets the stage for Franco's overhearing a conversation between border-guards which strikes fear into his heart because he suspects that they are describing Ombretta's tragedy. Mention of the familiar details of the landscape has intensified the reader's participation in Franco's growing excitement as he nears home, and his still veiled fear that Ombretta may be, not sick, but already dead becomes all the more real.

Along with detailed description, where called for, Fogazzaro uses lively conversation. He does not have such a large proportion of dialogue to narrative prose as does, say, the Anglo-American humorist P. G. Wodehouse;[16] frequently, he will introduce a brief exchange of a few sentences in the midst of a long passage describing his characters' perceptions or reactions to a situation. As we shall see in the next chapter, Fogazzaro uses local dialect wherever a character would normally speak dialect rather than standard Italian, thereby attaining greater faithfulness to reality as actually experienced.

The over-all effect of Fogazzaro's narrative technique is to create in the reader the feeling of having lived through the various events and experiences narrated, so that they are as alive in his or her memory as they were in Fogazzaro's remembrances or imagination.[17] The selective realism thus achieved is of course limited to a particular time (the second half of the nineteenth century and the beginning of the twentieth) and region (northern Italy and adjacent territories) because those were the time and place which Fogazzaro himself knew. His works are thereby rendered all the more valuable, as a portrayal in depth, rather than in breadth, of that particular phase of Italian history and mores.

CHAPTER 8

Music, Language, and Style

I Music

IN all of Fogazzaro's novels, and in a number of his short stories, music is so interwoven with the action and with the emotions of the characters as to constitute an essential part of the story.[1] Some authors of this period make very little use of music (for example, Verga); others, such as d'Annunzio, use it as an element of show and splendor. In Fogazzaro's work, however, music is both a theme in its own right and an accompaniment to the development of the action of his stories and an expression of the psychology of his characters. A Fogazzaro novel without any mention of music would no longer be a Fogazzaro novel.

Fogazzaro was an ardent music-lover, and his home was the scene of a great deal of music-making—a domestic activity which was much more common, in the days before gramophones and radios, than it is nowadays. He himself, although not a skilled performer, had at least been exposed to instruction on the piano and played some as an amateur. His father and (at least in the earlier years of their marriage) his wife showed considerable ability; their daughter Maria inherited notable skill as a pianist from her mother and from Mariano Fogazzaro Sr. A number of professional musicians were among Fogazzaro's closest friends, especially the eccentric Neapolitan cellist Gaetano Braga, the composer Arrigo Boito, and, later, the Roman composer Giovanni Sgambati.

Fogazzaro's tastes in music were markedly different from those of his Italian contemporaries. His major preferences were for the German Romantics and for "musica antica," which to him meant that of Italian, French, and German composers of the seventeenth and eighteenth centuries. Schumann was his favorite, to judge by the number of times (twelve) his works are mentioned in Fogazzaro's eight novels and the six short stories and eight poems in which

109

music is involved. Beethoven, Bellini, Pergolesi, and Bach follow,
with seven or more mentions each. Fogazzaro also refers to works
by a number of others, twenty-three in all. Naturally, the mere
number of passages in which a composer is mentioned does not
necessarily show Fogazzaro's attitude towards him, favorable or
otherwise. Verdi, for instance, is given only passing mention (occasionally with somewhat contemptuous implications) in six
passages, whereas Mendelssohn is mentioned in only five, but
favorably in four of them.[2] Meyerbeer is mentioned at three points
in *Malombra*, in all of which he constitutes a major enthusiasm of
Marina in her incipient insanity.

There are a total of one hundred seventy-three passages in Fogazzaro's fiction and poetry in which music is mentioned, of which
twenty-eight are relatively long. The introduction of music into
these twenty-eight passages is not just incidental; music plays an
important part either in advancing an essential step in the action of
the story or in establishing a background against which the action is
set. For the most part, Fogazzaro's references to music are serious
and elevate the tone of his scenes. A fair number of the one hundred seventy-three passages—thirty-three, or nearly a fifth—are,
however, humorous. In *Piccolo mondo moderno*, a minor character
named Bisata puts himself forward as a candidate for a post in the
town band, introducing himself at one point as *uno che suona il
pelittone in fa bemolle* "one who plays the pelittone [a rare type of
bass cornet] in F flat", and later as *quelo che sona el pelittone in mi*
"he who plays the pelittone in E". The humor resides both in the
instrument he plays and in his discrepant descriptions of it as in F
flat and in E. The whole of the short story "R. Schumann (dall'op.
68)" is a self-satire on Fogazzaro's part, and all eleven references to
the cellist Lazzaro Chieco involve some eccentricity on his part.

Most of Fogazzaro's references to music involve some specific activity, usually a performance by one or more characters in the story.
Instrumental performances outnumber vocal by almost three to
one, and—as might be expected from an author with Fogazzaro's
musical training and activities—the piano outnumbers all other in-
struments put together. Improvisation is mentioned only eight
times, but in *Miranda, Piccolo mondo antico,* and *Leila* it plays an
important rôle in casting light on the psychology of the main
characters. The conditions under which music is performed in
Fogazzaro's fiction are almost always domestic, including even the
two relatively large gatherings at Jeanne and Carlino Dessalles'
home at Villa Diedo in *Piccolo mondo moderno*. The only mention

of concerts is mildly unfavorable: in *Daniele Cortis*, the old senator Clenezzi admires and is grateful to Èlena because, among other reasons, she "never inflicted concert-tickets on him". The six instances of choral singing all take place under solemn circumstances; in two places (in *Piccolo mondo antico* and *Il santo*) they foreshadow death, and, in the next to the last episode of *Leila*, Benedetto's followers sing the *De Profundis* on the boat which is carrying his mortal remains to their last resting-place in Valsolda.

When we turn to the actual compositions which Fogazzaro mentions, identifiable either by name or by composer, and to the manner in which they are performed—vocally or instrumentally—we find a slight paradox. Although the total number of references to instrumental performances is, as we have seen, far greater than those of other kinds, the specific pieces mentioned are performed in almost exactly equal measure vocally (thirty-four) and instrumentally (thirty-three). This discrepancy is due to the fact that a great many mentions of instrumental performances do not specify the particular composition involved, and that a surprisingly high proportion of the compositions mentioned are operatic arias, mostly from eighteenth- and early nineteenth-century works. These works are performed, in Fogazzaro's fiction (as they probably were in his own home), in part vocally but also instrumentally—usually, as might be expected, on the piano. This anomaly, in its turn, is due to the fact that Fogazzaro's major music-making characters (especially Marina in *Malombra*, Franco in *Piccolo mondo antico*, and Marcello and Lelia in *Leila*) are pianists.

Fogazzaro's relation to the opera—which was in his time, as earlier, a dominant feature of Italian musical life—deserves special attention. Italian opera has always alternated passages of dramatic exposition (usually in *recitativo secco*) with arias expressing emotional states. For this reason, Fogazzaro's characters are fond of operatic arias with which they can identify their own feelings and by means of which they can express them, either in song or on the piano. Yet public musical activites—performances of not only operas, but also symphonies, instrumental trios or quartets, or large choral works—are almost entirely absent from Fogazzaro's fiction. Even Beethoven and Bach appear almost wholly as composers of solos or duets. Fogazzaro's characters, in general, live their inner lives and have their most intense feelings in the privacy of their homes and personal contacts, and their performances of music and their reactions to it follow the same pattern.[3]

Many of the passages in which music is mentioned are short and the part music plays in them is casual; others are longer and music has great importance in them. Music becomes a central part of the action (typically, some-one plays or sings and thereby exerts an influence on some-one else) or furnishes a background either corresponding or contrasting to the emotional tone of the action. In some passages, the music or the making of music serves to characterize; in others, it sets the emotional tone of a scene—the mood of the characters or their relationships to each other. *Leila* is the story with the largest number of long, important passages of this type (six); *Malombra, Piccolo mondo antico,* and *Piccolo mondo moderno* each have three; *Daniele Cortis* has only two, and *Il santo* just one.[4]

In the story "R. Schumann (dall'op. 68)", Donna Valentina recognizes that music is "a language without a dictionary and without a grammar, such that it cannot be translated instantly and with certainty".[5] Throughout his fiction, Fogazzaro, nevertheless, treated music as a vehicle for conveying meanings of a wholly emotional type—his characters' loves, sorrows, religious aspirations (especially in *Leila*), and (in the case of Marina in *Malombra*) frustrations and hatreds. Fogazzaro's lecture *Il dolore nell'arte* ("Sorrow in Art") is often cited in this connection, with his extensive discussion of the first movement of Beethoven's "Moonlight" sonata as a supreme exemplification of the power of music to express feelings beyond the reach of words. Some critics have been misled by the fact that Fogazzaro's characters are so frequently both musical and emotional, and consider them as "purely emotional" types, incapable of any other kind of behavior.

It must be pointed out, however, that in the first place not all of Fogazzaro's major characters are musically inclined. Foremost among these are his two reformers, Daniele Cortis and Franco Maironi. There is, in fact, a marked correlation between practicality and absence of music in Fogazzaro's fiction. Music is not mentioned at all in the middle third of *Il santo,* when Benedetto is in contact with the practical world of peasants, upper-class society, church, and government. He is described at one point as being so unmusical as not to be able even to strike a chord on the piano.

In the second place, not all of Fogazzaro's musically inclined people are romantically emotional. The dictatorial abbot of *Il santo,* who expels Benedetto, is highly musical, a good performer on the piano, and an admirer of Mozart in the best Fogazzarian manner. Carlino Dessalle is rather less disagreeable, but still somewhat affected in his *fin-de-siècle* aestheticism—but he is highly musical and shares all of Fogazzaro's enthusiasm for "musica antica." Even in his main characters, there are degrees of musicality. Luisa Maironi and Jeanne Dessalle, to mention only two, are considerably less advanced in their musical understanding and in their reaction to music than are, say, Èlena and Lelia. Fogazzaro's sense of humor, which is never far from the surface, also keeps his normal correlation of music and heightened emotion from deliquescing into sentimentality. Thus, for instance, when Franco and Luisa, in *Piccolo mondo antico*, are out boating on the lake, she sings a Donizetti aria, which Franco interprets as an expression of her desire for a more perfect union in their marriage. Immediately thereafter, they hear the aria "aped" by a bassoon from another boat, in which friends are coming to visit them.

By far the greater part of Fogazzaro's mentions of music fall under the heading of direct description; only a relatively small proportion of them are involved in similes or metaphors. There are only four similes, in two of which a broken-down old instrument serves as a term of comparison for a person's voice or mood, and fourteen metaphors. Most of his imagery involving music has emotional overtones. The only instances where his metaphors are non-emotional are the five in *Piccolo mondo moderno*. This absence of emotion in the metaphors in this novel is part of Fogazzaro's technique in conveying the dryness and emptiness of contemporary upper-class small-town society in contrast with Piero Maironi's developing religious devotion.

In some instances, a particular piece of music is associated with a given person or situation, thus reflecting an aspect of character or of the action. The clearest of these associations is that of Marina with Meyerbeer's *Robert le Diable;* her choice of this music corresponds to her ungovernable, wayward temperament. The Pergolesi aria *Se cerca, se dice* is associated with Èlena's and Daniele's renunciation of love in *Daniele Cortis;* Schumann's song *Ich hab' im Traum geweinet* ("I wept in my dream") and Schubert's *Heidenröslein* ("Wild Rose"), with the narrator's love for Violet in *Il Mistero del Poeta*. In some instances, the contents of a certain piece are appropriate for a particular occasion. A fantasia on Verdi's *I vespri siciliani* ("The Sicilian Vespers") fits the presence of the Barone di Santa Giulia at a gathering at Villa Carré; the band plays the chorus of exiles from Verdi's *Nabucco* ("Nebuchadnezzar") just before Èlena leaves for her exile at Cefalù. The best known of all Fogaz-

zaro's associations of songs with people is the repeated use of the
Rossini aria *Ombretta sdegnosa del Mississipi* in *Piccolo mondo an-
tico*, from which Maria Maironi gets her nickname "Ombretta
Pipì."

Fogazzaro's use of music in his fiction is, in short, quite individual. For his characters, reaction to either their own or others'
performance of music is a natural accompaniment, in general, to
heightened emotional sensitivity—one of the ways in which intense
longing, primarily but by no means exclusively sexual love, is
manifested. The natural medium of the narrator's art is the
linguistic structure—sounds, grammar, lexicon—which he uses in
his story. In Fogazzaro's work, music forms an essential extension of
this medium, conveying meanings and emotions which are beyond
the expressive capacity of the structure of language.

II   *Language and Dialect*

In virtually every modern European or American society, a particular variety of language has come to be regarded as the favored
vehicle for literary use,[6] and is often considered as *the* language par
excellence. At the same time, other, less favored varieties of speech
are down-graded and treated as "mere" dialects, even though they
may continue to be used on all levels of society (as in northern Italy,
especially the Vèneto region) in every-day conversation. The distinction between *lingua* "language (par excellence)" and *dialetto*
"dialect" was established in the sixteenth and seventeenth centuries
in accordance with the then prevailing authoritarian trends, and has
persisted in Italy down to the present time. Schools and academies
have encouraged an unrealistic rigidity in maintaining this sharp
distinction, which has by no means died out in puristic circles.

During the nineteenth century, prejudices against the use of
dialect in literature began to decline, first of all in the English-
speaking world. In his novels dealing with Scottish life—such as
Rob Roy (1817), *The Antiquary* (1816), or *The Heart of Midlothian*
(1818)—Sir Walter Scott (1771 - 1832) introduced conversation in
"braid Scots" for two main purposes: to give his personages' speech
a homely, intimate, unpretentious character; and, at points of
heightened emotional tension, to emphasize the speakers' remarks.
Mark Twain (1835 - 1910) went even farther. In *The Adventures of
Tom Sawyer* (1876), almost all the conversation is in dialect, but the
third-person narration is in standard English. In *The Adventures of*

Huckleberry Finn (1884), however, almost all of the book is in dialect, since Huck narrates it in the first person.[7] Twain distinguished very carefully between seven varieties of local speech, thereby gaining far greater authenticity than if he had had his characters use an unrealistic standard English. In Italy, however, very few authors had dared, before the late nineteenth century, to write their stories in any but "pure" Italian. The greatest novelist of the first half of the century, Alessandro Manzoni (1785 - 1873), had in fact been so dissatisfied with the Milanese and Lombard regionalisms in the first version (1827) of his *I promessi sposi* ("The Betrothed") that he subjected his novel to an extensive revision to bring it in line with Florentine usage in its definitive form (1840 - 42).[8]

Fogazzaro was the first widely-read Italian novelist to use local dialect at all extensively in his fiction.[9] He began to do so only gradually. For his lyric poetry, *Miranda*, and the lyrically narrated *Mistero del poeta*, he used only standard Italian. Even in *Malombra*, there is relatively little dialect. Not until *Daniele Cortis* did Fogazzaro begin to introduce it to any extent, and his use of dialect is at its greatest in the first two novels of the Maironi tetralogy. There is relatively little in *Il santo*—which, as we have seen, is a novel of ideas rather than of manners—but he returns to a greater use of dialect in *Leila*. There is a fair amount in some short stories as well. We may say, in general, that there is a strong correlation between realism and the presence of dialect in the conversation of Fogazzaro's characters. He always uses standard Italian in the narration, except for the occasional introduction of a few individual words to refer to a personage or to an object for which a special dialectal term is needed. The particular dialect is always that which its user, in a given story, would have according to his region of origin: mostly Lombard (in the Valsolda) or Venetian (in or near Vicenza), occasionally Tuscan or Roman.

The function of dialect in Fogazzaro's stories is the same that it has in Scott. Especially in *Piccolo mondo antico*, a large part of the conversation is in dialect, even to the extent of having some personages speak in Lombard while others reply in the (very closely related) Venetian. Here and in *Piccolo mondo moderno*, Fogazzaro creates an intimate, homely atmosphere by recording his characters' speech exactly as it would have occurred in real life. On occasion, certain unsympathetic personages from other regions of Italy behave in an out-of-place fashion, which Fogazzaro emphasizes by giving their speech some dialectal characteristics. Thus, in *Daniele Cortis,* the Baron of Santa Giulia shows his Sicilian origin by putting the preposition *a* before a direct object, as is normal in Sicilian dialect. In *Piccolo mondo moderno,* an antipathetic Tuscan deputy betrays his origin by the presence of the "gorgia toscana"[10] in his speech.

Again as in Scott, dialect serves also to heighten the dramatic effect of a scene. In *Piccolo mondo antico,* the women of the town come to tell Luisa of Ombretta's drowning by screaming *Esüs Maria, sciora Lüisa!* "Jesus and Mary, Signora Luisa!". Later in the same novel, when the by-standers attempt to comfort Luisa by assuring her that Maria is now in Paradise, she replies, in Lombard dialect, *El mi Paradis l'è chi!* "My Paradise is here!". Characters of all social levels, from the peasants to the aristocrats, use dialect in Fogazzaro's stories where their real-life prototypes would have done so. Purists have objected to the presence of so much dialect, especially in his best-known novel, *Piccolo mondo antico,* which has the most conversation in dialect of all his stories. Such objections are out of place, both in general (since dialect is not intrinsically inferior to standard language) and as applied to Fogazzaro. His use of dialect is restricted to the passages where it would be appropriate, and in those passages it is highly effective.

Fogazzaro's standard Italian is that which was normal in the mid-nineteenth century, as found in the writings of his contemporaries such as Giovanni Verga, Salvatore Farina, Luigi Capuana, and many others. In his lyric poetry, he uses the normal license with regard to optional apocopation—the omission of a final vowel, as in *'dolor* for *dolore* "sorrow"—and archaic grammatical forms such as *vo* for *vado* "I go". In prose, Fogazzaro's grammatical forms and constructions are those of his time. Occasionally he uses words which are normal in the region of Vicenza but not in Tuscany, e.g., *piova* "rain"[11] instead of *pioggia.* On other occasions, he might use some particularly poetic word, such as *cémbalo* (a variant of *clavicémbalo,* usually "harpsichord"[12]) for "piano" in both his poetry and his personal correspondence. In these respects, his usage was no different from that of any normal speaker of Italian or any other modern standard language.

III *Style*

Fogazzaro's especial attention to music, and the all-pervasive rôle that music plays in most of his fiction, has led many observers to consider "musicality" the major characteristic of his style.[13] This and similar terms, however, are not sufficiently clear in their reference to be defined with anything resembling objectivity, and hence to be useful in further stylistic analysis.

There have been many definitions of style. The one which I have found most useful in dealing with literature is "the use which an author makes of the resources afforded by his artistic medium—language—and the means which he employs to achieve the effects which his work has upon the reader or hearer". To analyze style effectively and at the same time objectively, it is helpful to distinguish, with Michael Riffaterre,[14] three factors which differentiate one author's style from another's: the specific devices which are used to obtain a particular effect, or *stylistic devices;* the immediate context in which each stylistic device occurs, or *stylistic context;* and the over-all background against which stylistic devices occur in their contexts, or *stylistic background.* By distinguishing these three factors within each text, studied in and for itself, it is possible to isolate and identify the stylistic individuality of each author without needing to have recourse to extrinsic criteria such as the usage of other authors or the general linguistic norm of a speech-community. On the other hand, if data concerning other authors' usage or the speech-community as a whole are available, they can constitute valuable additional sources of information.

The types of stylistic devices, contexts, and backgrounds differ according to the genre of literature involved and the effect which the author produces (intentionally or unintentionally) in the reader. In serious prose works aiming at arousing a more or less intense emotional reaction, the background will in general be a formal standard type of usage,[15] the context relatively extended, and the devices consonant with their backgrounds and contexts. In humor, on the other hand, the background may or may not be serious. There may or may not be a discrepancy between the background and the context of a humorous stylistic device. The device itself, however, will normally be unexpected and will, in one way or another, make us laugh because of its lack of consonance with what we expect in the particular context or against the particular background involved.[16] In poetry, an author further commits himself in advance to observe certain limitations with regard to meter, rhyme, and the like, in accordance with the possibilities afforded by the structure of his language.[17]

Fogazzaro provides us, in his novels and short stories, with many examples of both serious and humorous style, often alternating in the same work. In both his serious and humorous writing, the background is the same, as observed in the previous section: the formal standard Italian of the second half of the nineteenth century. How he varies this material to achieve his effects would in itself furnish the subject for an entire volume.[18] Here, we shall limit the discussion to one short story, *Un'idea di Ermes Torranza* (1882), and to one particular stylistic device as used at the end, as well as to remarks concerning his intercalated humorous passages.

The final sentence of the story, occurring both after the heroine Bianca and her husband Emilio have been reconciled, and she has felt that Torranza's spirit has taken final leave of her and the world, is simply *Bianca tornò a piegargli il viso sul petto* "Bianca bowed her face on his breast again". The stylistic device used here is the occurrence of the two nouns *il viso* "the face" and *il petto* "the breast" without any modifying descriptive adjectives, giving an effect of quiet simplicity to the ending of the story. It derives this effect from the stylistic context, in which Fogazzaro uses most of his nouns with one or more descriptive adjectives, phrases introduced by a preposition, or clauses modifying them. A rough count of the nouns in the first six paragraphs of this story shows a total of one hundred eight-five, of which only forty, or twenty-one and one-tenth percent, are not accompanied by a descriptive adjective, phrase, or clause.

The position of the descriptive adjective is also important in Fogazzaro's prose style. What Dwight L. Bolinger has observed for Spanish[19] is true for the other Romance languages as well: an adjective placed after a noun tells the hearer or reader that the quality indicated by the adjective is being contrasted with some other possible quality that might characterize what is referred to by the noun. An adjective placed before a noun, on the other hand, indicates no such contrast, and therefore tells the hearer that the quality referred to by the adjective is inherent, not subject to doubt or alternatives. Thus, for instance, in Italian, *l'erba verde* means "the grass which is green" (and not, say, brown or yellow), whereas *la verde erba* simply refers to grass which is by its nature green, without contrasting it with grass of any other color. In the first six paragraphs of *Un'idea di Ermes Torranza*, Fogazzaro has a remarkably high proportion of adjectives placed before the nouns they modify. Fifty-two nouns, or twenty-eight and two-tenths percent of the total, have preposed adjectives, whereas fifty-nine nouns, or thirty-two and four-tenths percent, have one or more postposed adjectives.[20] This proportion of preposed adjectives is markedly higher than is normal in Italian usage (written or spoken). We thus find such expressions as *Il solitario palazzo* "the solitary palace," *la lunga scalinata* "the long stairway," *altre cùpide mani* "other eager hands," and *le colossali piante* "the colossal plants." In many such phrases, Fogazzaro has the noun both preceded and followed by an adjective or other type of modifier, as in *i nostri freddi critici corretti* "our cold, correct critics," or *quei trèmoli pennacchi giallo-rossicci* "those quivering yellow-reddish tree-tops." Since, in Bolinger's words, the preposed adjectives tell us that the qualities they refer to are "to be expected" or "taken for granted," this linguistic technique is one of the means whereby Fogazzaro commands the reader's belief—outside of the latter's awareness, and through the semantics of grammatical structure—in the reality of what is being described.

If we contrast the figures for *Torranza* with those obtained from a rough count of nouns with descriptive adjectives in the almost contemporary short story *Fra le corde d'un contrabasso* ("Between the Strings of a Double-Bass," 1882) by Salvatore Farina (1846 - 1918), we find an interesting difference. In the first six paragraphs of *Fra le corde* we find one hundred fifty-five nouns, of which only forty-six or thirty percent, are accompanied by descriptive adjectives. Of these forty-six, thirty-two (twenty-one percent) have the adjective postposed; only fourteen (nine percent) have them preposed. The resultant effect of sobriety and objectivity helps to establish the light, humorous, and basically unemotional tone of Farina's story.

The length of paragraphs and sentences, and the structure of the latter (simple, complex, compound, or compound-complex), are also interesting. In the first six paragraphs of *Torranza* there are forty-one sentences and one thousand two hundred twenty-two words, with an average of twenty nine and eight-tenths words per sentence. The paragraphs therefore average two hundred three and sixty-six hundredths words each. Paragraphs two and five are short, containing only two sentences each; paragraphs one and three contain five each; but four and six have twelve and fifteen sentences, respectively. There is no major correlation between paragraph- and sentence-length. Of the two longest sentences, that with eighty-seven words occurs in paragraph three, which is short, and that with ninety words, in the longest paragraph, number six. Of the forty-one sentences, thirteen are both compound and complex; seven more are complex; and nine more are compound. Twelve sentences (twenty-nine percent) are neither, and of these, seven are quotations in direct or indirect discourse. These latter are also much the shortest, averaging nine words apiece. In general, Fogazzaro's sentences quoted from conversations are very much shorter and less complicated than those of his narration.

When we compare these figures with those obtained from a similar count of the first six paragraphs of Farina's *Fra le corde*, we find that Farina has slightly longer sentences (thirty-two and twenty-five hundredths words), but only one hundred fifty and five-tenths words per paragraph, making nine hundred three words altogether, with only twenty-eight sentences. Of these, six are compound, seven are complex, and nine are compound-complex, making twenty-two all. The six which are neither compound, complex, or compound-complex form twenty-one and five-tenths percent of the twenty-eight sentences. Some of Fogazzaro's paragraphs are considerably longer than Farina's, but they are skillfully alternated with shorter ones; the same holds true of the sentences. Farina has only one sentence of eighty-five words, but relatively few short sentences (three altogether, of five, seven, and seven words respectively). Fogazzaro's paragraphs give, therefore, greater information, especially—with his large number of preposed adjectives—concerning the "to-be-expected" and hence inherent attributes of the persons and things he describes.

In *Un'idea di Ermes Torranza*, the reader is left at the end with four major impressions, aside from the outline of the story itself: night, mist, autumnal decline leading to death, and possible influence of the spirits of the dead on the actions of the living. Fogazzaro carefully sets the stage for these impressions and imprints them on the reader's memory by skillfully introducing words and phrases which will suggest them. The very first sentence contains a reference to the Horatian tag *fabulaeque Manes* "the storied spirits of the dead," which is soon amplified by the complete quotation, containing the word *nox* "night." The second sentence contains the word *autunno* "autumn," which recurs several times later. Bianca's separation from Emilio took place in September, and lasted two months, into November. The white-bearded Torranza is in his sixties, and dies in the course of the story, promising to communicate with her after his passing. She receives his letter just as night is falling, and the white mist is rising around Monte San Donà and shutting it off from the rest of the world. From this point on, darkness and mist furnish the background, with the words *notte* "night" and *nebbia* "mist" recurring several times, varied by such synonymic expressions as *il triste ocèano bianco* "the sad white ocean" or *il suo vapor denso* "its thick vapor." At the end, Bianca does not know whether or not to believe that Torranza's spirit has, by closing the sheet of the song over his portrait, made its final adieu to her and disappeared into the darkness.

Torranza also has a certain dose of Fogazzarian humor, of a satirical kind, in the descriptions of Bianca's parents and their actions, and in the account of the visit from the town gossips who first tell Bianca of the old poet's death. Her father is constantly referred to, ironically, as *il nòbile sior Beneto* "the noble Mr. Beneto" (note the position of the adjective *nòbile*) as Fogazzaro describes his mean and stingy actions. Bianca's father refers to her mother as "that saintly woman"; but Fogazzaro tells us that the latter was "a saint by compulsion" under the petty tyranny of her husband. She was "secretly glad that the girl had not bent her neck under the yoke and had not let herself be made a saint like her." In describing the group, Fogazzaro brings together comically incongruous elements:

> It was the Dalla Carretta family with their guests, a little archaeological museum of long black shawls, of over-ornamented bonnets, of ecclesiastical stockings and tassels, of insipid faces: pestiferous people who came once a year, as a matter of propriety, to sit in a circle and look at each other for awhile without knowing what to say; after which an old servant in a gray jacket would come in very decorously to bring the coffee and cakes which the gallant Beneto would serve, together with his little jokes which were always the same, and at which the company laughed regularly every year in the same key and rhythm. To miss a beautiful November sunset for these people! Bianca could not stand them; they made it impossible for her to breathe.

In their conversation, the guests mingle their chit-chat about the late poet with inconsequential actions, which contrast sharply with Bianca's reaction:

> "I don't know," Canon Businello said to her between sips of coffee, "I don't know whether you've heard the bad news . . ."
> "No. What news . . . ?" Bianca answered in a whisper.
> "Ah, to be sure," said two or three low voices. "Ah, yes, to be sure."
> "Poor Torranza, poor man . . ." the Canon added mournfully, dipping the last piece of cake in his coffee.
> Bianca felt a contraction in her heart and a cold tingling on her face, and could not utter a word.

"Unfortunately," said the monsignore, moving his cup around to dissolve the sugar which had remained at the bottom. "Deceased, yes . . ." He emptied his cup and added, sighing, "Last night, at half past eleven."

Fogazzaro is very sparing in his use of imagery. In all of *Un'idea di Ermes Torranza*, there are only five similes, six metaphors (of which four refer to the "sea" of mist), and three symbols: the poplars losing their leaves and a leaf circling lazily to the ground as symbols of death, and the mist on the ground with the moon faintly visible above as a symbol of the relation between earthly and spiritual life. The few similes and metaphors that he uses are straightforward and immediate, drawn from the world as it is perceived by human senses—mostly plants, animals, features of the landscape. The objects with which a person, thing, or emotion is compared have, in general, a close, easily perceptible relation to the thing being compared. Fogazzaro does not introduce far-fetched similes or daring metaphors.[21] Thus, he tells us that Torranza compared Bianca, when she was fifteen, to "a smiling little poplar"; that the music she was playing entered her heart "like an invisible river"; or that Beneto "whinnied a guttural laugh, with his mouth closed." This same paucity and directness of imagery characterizes the rest of Fogazzaro's writing, even *Il mistero del poeta*, the one among his novels which might be thought to offer the greatest scope for flights of the imagination.

The "musicality" which some critics have seen in Fogazzaro's style derives, therefore, very largely from the greater extent to which his adjectival style conveys emotional over-tones, coupled with the imagery of nature conveyed through impressions of sight and sound, which awakens affective responses in the hearer in harmony with the situations Fogazzaro is describing. This phenomenon holds true quite without regard to the actual mention of music, and occurs even in long stretches—such as the middle third of *Il santo*, or in a few short stories like *Eden Anto*—in which music as such is not present.

Fogazzaro's style is characterized by a contrast between the immediacy and exactitude with which he describes scenes and events, and the loftiness and inevitable indeterminacy of the spiritual aspirations of many of his personages. His use of the grammatical and semantic resources of Italian to achieve this two-fold purpose is highly skillful.[22] Fogazzaro is thus enabled to present simultaneously a background which is, as it were, etched sharply on the narrator's memory and a foreground in which thoroughly individualized personages live out the ritual of their regular existence[23] and gradually, through their actions and relations to each other, come to face situations of crisis. As in real life, these crises do not always reach a definitive solution. As we proceed from *Miranda* and *Malombra*, in which sudden, unexpected death puts a sharp end to the action, to *Daniele Cortis*, we are already presented with a more open-ended resolution of the dramatic conflict. In *Il mistero del poeta*, Violet dies, but the poet feels that her spirit is still alive and that he is in permanent communion with her. All of the novels of the Maironi tetralogy have open-ended conclusions, even *Leila*, whose final message is that life must go on, even when hope has been dashed. Given Fogazzaro's beliefs and attitudes towards the relation of material and spiritual existence, his writing—in the characters he portrays and in his use of Italian language and style to portray them—is the most efficacious means that any author could have used.

CHAPTER 9

Fogazzaro's Message to Italy

I *Posthumous Reputation*

FOGAZZARO'S reputation was at its highest in the decade between the publication of *Piccolo mondo antico* (1896) and that of *Il santo* (1905). His novels had aroused extensive and lively public interest, for both their artistic merits and their moral and religious content. His support of the movement for reform in the Catholic church had earned him the allegiance of the very large group among the faithful who wished to see a renewal or an *aggiornamento* (to use the term of half a century later) of their religion. To many, religion seemed to have been unfortunately and needlessly deprived of its ethical and spiritual content. Some favorable critics had already assigned Fogazzaro a place among the greatest Italian novelists, together with Manzoni, Verga, and Nievo.[1] Fogazzaro had become internationally famous, and his works were beginning to be translated into French, English, German, and other languages.

Beginning with the publication of *Il santo*, however, and its official condemnation in 1906, Fogazzaro's reputation began to decline. The first source of denigration was, as might have been expected, the ultra-conservative clerical group which at the time was dominant in the Catholic church. For a time, up to the encyclical *Pascendi* in 1907 and for a year or two thereafter, there was extensive discussion of the pros and cons of reform, into which Fogazzaro entered to a certain extent.[2] These debates ceased by 1910, however, and from that time on, Pius X's condemnation of the modernist positions was regarded as definitive and permanently unappealable. This attitude served literary critics, in their discussions of Fogazzaro and his works, as an excuse for neglecting his views on religion and morals, and for regarding them as intrusive elements, at best negligible and at worst harmful to the novelist's art. This at-

124

titude lasted until and even extended beyond the Second Vatican Council. Even such a favorable critic as Piero Nardi was able to refer to the religious and political elements in Fogazzaro's works as "topics which are now out of date", and Emilio Scampini could say "the problems which Fogazzaro discussed were certainly lofty, but have no interest any longer nowadays".[3]

Negative judgments on the literary merits of Fogazzaro's work also began to appear during his life-time. The first critic to raise objections was Benedetto Croce[4] who considered Fogazzaro, along with others, to exemplify what he regarded as "insincerity," and an inadmissible mixture of "artistic" and "extra-artistic" elements. The accusation of insincerity was based on Croce's and others' view of the moral problems that are treated in *Daniele Cortis* and *Piccolo mondo moderno*. It seemed to these critics that Fogazzaro, although preaching the loftiest ideals of morality and self-sacrifice, was hypocritical in giving, at the same time, an excessively attractive picture of the pleasure deriving from temptation. Fogazzaro also appeared to be defending a kind of "spiritual adultery" which was, if anything, even more immoral than illicit physical love. (These critics, however, do not make clear how an author is to portray the overcoming of temptation effectively without describing the temptation itself.)

Croce and his followers—who have constituted the dominant school of literary criticism in twentieth-century Italy—insisted on a sharp distinction between "poetry" and "non-poetry." Literature, according to Crocean doctrines, should not concern itself with such "extra-artistic" topics as religion, politics, or morals because they are not poetic (i.e., appealing to the aesthetic sense) and hence clash with what is poetic. Thus, for instance, it has been a commonplace of Crocean criticism to praise certain sections of Dante's *Divina Commedia* for their poetic beauty, such as the Francesca da Rìmini episode in Canto V of the *Inferno*, but to condemn other sections because they are expositions of encyclopaedic knowledge or abstruse theological dogma (especially in the *Paradiso*).[5] From the Crocean point of view, therefore, Fogazzaro's concern with "extra-artistic" matters constituted a fundamental flaw in the aesthetic quality of his work.[6]

With writers or composers whose works arouse strong emotional responses, it often happens that they awaken very great enthusiasm in some readers or listeners (especially young ones), amounting virtually to infatuation. Later, these persons, on reaching greater maturity of understanding and critical approach, not only lose their enthusiasm but turn violently against their former idols. This has happened to such composers as Rachmaninov and Delius, and, in literature, to authors of the type of Kipling, Eichendorff, or Victor Hugo. In Italian literature, no author has suffered as much as Fogazzaro from the hostile criticism of ex-fans,[7] who see in his work only the aspects which earlier aroused their enthusiasm and which they later have come to dislike. Thus, for example, when Viola affirms that Fogazzaro's characters are "purely emotional types," he sees, not the personages as their creator actually portrayed them in their psychological complexity, but simply the one aspect that he is able to perceive in them, and against which he rebelled in the course of his disillusionment. For critics of the "ex-fan" type, their writings on Fogazzaro are essentially autobiographical, representing part of their process of emotional catharsis.

Before the First World War, Fogazzaro's desire for social reform and general sympathy with the less radical side of the socialist movement[8] saved him from all but a small amount of criticism from the leftists.[9] During the Fascist era, no left-oriented criticism was permitted. After the Second World War, Communists and fellow-travellers began, as part of their general critical activity, to examine Fogazzaro's work from the view-point of Marxist orthodoxy. As might be expected, he was subjected to strong criticisms because his "ideology" was different from and in many respects opposed to theirs. Marxist critics such as Piromalli,[10] Trombatore,[11] and Salinari[12] did not, indeed, make the Crocean mistake of regarding Fogazzaro's political and religious beliefs as merely so much un-aesthetic and hence irrelevant impedimenta. They at least took them seriously. For the Marxist critics, however, Fogazzaro was to blame for expressing the ideals of the nineteenth-century bourgeoisie. He did not foresee the future in the only terms acceptable to the Marxists—those of the proletarian revolutionary movement—and (they said, wrongly) was oriented more towards the past than towards the future.[13]

Fortunately, Freudian psychology, aside from a brief discussion in the Piccionis' book,[14] has generally not been brought to bear on Fogazzaro. One critic did indeed, when discussing the relation between Jeanne Dessalle and Noemi d'Arxel in the early chapters of *Il Santo,* speak of them as "lesbianizing in religion." Such an interpretation is of course grossly erroneous, since in those times women exchanged caresses, especially slight ones such as those between

Jeanne and Noemi, as an indication of wholly innocent relationships. Nothing could have been farther from Fogazzaro's intentions than to introduce a factor of homosexuality into a situation demanding a progressive victory over all sensual elements. [15]

In addition to criticism from the four specific groups just discussed—clericals, Croceans, Marxists, ex-fans—there are certain more general factors that have militated against recognition of Fogazzaro's merits. Modern attitudes towards sex-relations render it quite difficult, especially for members of the European (and, nowadays, also the American) intelligentsia to understand the notion of self-restraint or even of the existence of any kind of problem in such matters. Kinsey-type statistics ae not necessary as a basis for the observation that it is not sexual libertinism, but abstinence, which nowadays arouses surprise and (often) contempt in intellectual circles. Cynicism and hostility towards inherited moral standards make it easy for many to make fun of the long *crises de conscience* of Daniele Cortis or of Piero Maironi, and hence of Fogazzaro's own personal inner conflicts.

Romanticism, too, is very much out of fashion in the modern world—at least, the type of romanticism which involves the unabashed portrayal of the love-emotion. In Italy, especially, authors of the late nineteenth and early twentieth century whose characters gave too free a rein to their sentiments have automatically been classed as "decadent," with all the unfavorable connotations that this term normally has, but with a peculiar twist to its meaning. In general, for a writer to be termed "decadent," he has to manifest the following characteristics: rebellion against morality (Satanism, titanism, atheistic Prometheanism, exaggerated sexuality, or other forms of mental unbalance) and against classical form; the doctrine of "art for art's sake," leading to futurism and surrealism; and "all kinds of deformation, from the visual and plastic to the auditory effects of dissonance." [16] Fogazzaro of course shows none of these charactertistics, as can be seen immediately by comparing him with Baudelaire,[17] d'Annunzio, Marinetti,[18] Palazzeschi,[19] or any other true decadent. Yet, many Italian critics have allowed Fogazzaro's romantic emphasis on intensely felt emotion and inner psychological conflict to suffice for tacking the facile label "decadent" onto his works.

In addition to modern aversion to moral standards and romanticism, certain specifically Italian phenomena have contributed to the decline of Fogazzaro's reputation in Italy until recent years.

Relatively few Italians, in the nearly three quarters of a century
since the encyclical *Pascendi* of 1907, are inclined to consider
seriously the need for internal reform in the Catholic church. It has
become very difficult for the Italian "man in the street" to conceive
of the possibility of a serious criticism of the Church that is not at
the same time an absolute opposition, or an effective renewal that is
not complete destruction. Many Italians now regard the Catholic
religion as either a congeries of superficial, meaningless ritual practices or as an object meriting total indifference.[20] An author who
takes his Catholicism as seriously as Fogazzaro, and especially one
who makes church-reform a central issue, is not likely to seem
meaningful or "relevant" to a large section of the twentieth-century
reading public.

Nationalism, too, has played a rôle in diminishing the esteem in
which Fogazzaro has been held in Italy. He was not at all fond of
the Italian literature and music of his time. To the grandiose
rhetoric which characterized the most popular authors of his
day—in the poetry of, say, Carducci[21] or d'Annunzio—he preferred
the simplicity of previous epochs or the contemporary art of Germany, France, and England. Even before 1914, defensive
nationalism and hostility to foreign influence had begun to make
themselves evident in Italian intellectual life,[22] leading in the end to
Italian intervention in the First World War and to Fascism—nor did
it disappear after Fascism was overthrown. Especially in official,
Crocean literary criticism, this cultural navel-contemplation has led
to the over-valuation of "purely" Italian authors, e.g., Verga or
Moravia,[23] in preference to less exclusively nationally-oriented
writers such as Fogazzaro or Svevo.[24]

A third factor in the situation has been purism of various types:
linguistic, aesthetic, and psychological. Ever since the Renaissance,
the linguistic usage of Tuscany, and particularly of Florence, has
been held up as an exclusive model for literary writing. With the extension of standard Italian to all the regions of Italy, and with the
gradual development, first of primary and later of secondary educa-
tion, those who favored the standard language felt insecure with
regard to the use of dialect, particularly in prestigious literature.
Ironically, Fogazzaro's most famous work, *Piccolo mondo antico*, is
also, as we have seen, the one that contains the most conversation in
dialect. Hence Fogazzaro's writing has been considered "impure,"
particularly by Crocean critics, for whom dialect is by its very

nature unbeautiful and hence inadmissible, no matter what its dramatic or narrative function.

Aesthetic purism consists essentially in setting up certain standards *a priori,* and condemning whatever does not conform to predetermined criteria of what is beautiful. In seventeenth- and eighteenth-century Italy, these criteria were those of neoclassicism, as set down by sixteenth-century literary critics and law-givers.[25] Neoclassicism is dead, but its place has been taken by the equally absolutist but much vaguer abstract theories of the beautiful and the poetic as propounded by Croce and his school.[26] Looked at objectively, these doctrines have no absolute validity; they are determined wholly by the personal preferences of each individual critic and by the prejudices of the culture in which he has grown up. Crocean criticism has dominated the Italian literary scene since the beginning of the twentieth century, more so than in other countries. To go against Crocean aesthetic principles has been to a considerable extent regarded almost as a crime of treason against one's country. It is significant that Fogazzaro has been, on the whole, much more popular, and that his popularity has been more lasting, with non-Italian than with Italian critics—for instance, with McKenzie,[27] Portier,[28] Leo,[29] or Rheinfelder.[30]

Some critics have also indulged in the third type of purism which might be labelled "psychological." Taking Manzoni as the supreme Italian novelist, and his *I promessi sposi* ("The Betrothed") as the yardstick against which all other novels are to be measured, his characters have been praised for their simplicity, faith, innocence, and naïveté.[31] D'Annunzio is praised for his characters' absence of inhibitions or hesitations, especially in their direct drive for the satisfaction of their sexual desires. Fogazzaro's personages show inner conflicts, have *crises de conscience,* struggle against their instincts and strive for higher goals; hence both they and their creator are judged to be not only weak but somehow impure. In fact, of course, Fogazzaro's characters conquer their weaknesses and become notably purified in the course of their development; furthermore, he himself could never be considered "impure" in his personal life, morals, or religion.

As a result of the criticisms directed at Fogazzaro's work by the four groups just discussed—clericals, Croceans, Marxists, exfans—and largely on the basis of the several types of purism which we have enumerated, most current criticism and historiography of

Italian literature gives an incomplete and distorted picture of his achievement. He is usually caricatured as decadent,[32] confused over philosophical matters, a dilettante in such unaesthetic and hence unliterary fields as religion and biology, vague in his mystical aspirations, the creator of characters who are tormented by a half-spiritual, half-sensual religiosity, and the author of only one book of any value at all (naturally, *Piccolo mondo antico*).[33] Often, critics and writers of text-books make such inaccurate statements as that all Fogazzaro's characters reflect an "unlimited autobiographical approach" (*autobiografismo senza limiti*) on his part, or that he never shows any sense of humor in his treatment of music. Curiously, his works are still quite popular with the reading public, and films and television-dramas have been made from them (*Piccolo mondo antico, Malombra*).

II   *The Voice of Conscience*

Why, however, such a determined effort, with such obvious *parti pris*, on the part of so many Italian critics to "cut Fogazzaro down to size," to class him among the minor writers of the nineteenth century along with such authors as De Amicis[34] or Capuana,[35] and to dissuade the Italian public from reading and responding to his works? The answer lies, I think, in the fact that Fogazzaro, more than any other single Italian writer since Manzoni, has spoken with what might be termed the voice of conscience, reminding his readers of the obligations that Catholic Christianity and liberal democracy place upon anyone who takes them at all seriously. Naturally, those who are hostile to Catholicism, to the reform of the Catholic church, or to democracy interpreted in a liberal and at the same time Christian way, will do all they can to undercut the influence of such an author. Hence the enmity of the clericals in his own time and of the Marxists in later days. Both these groups object, not so much to the voice of conscience being heard, as to Fogazzaro's conscience, considering it the kind that they think ought not to be listened to. The Croceans' denigration of Fogazzaro derives from his exemplification of a type of beauty and poetry which in itself constitutes a disproof of their narrow, aprioristic, absolutistic dogmas of aesthetics, and from their belief that the voice of conscience has no place in literature. The "ex-fans"—some of them Crocean, some Marxist, and some both—have added the intensity of their emotional revulsion against their former idol.

In recent years, the situation has changed, most of all because of the new atmosphere prevailing since the Second Vatican Council (1960 - 62) and the beginnings of the *aggiornamento* or "updating" called for by the same Àngelo Roncalli (Pope John XXIII) who had been the secretary of the bishop of Bèrgamo at the time of the "Modernist" crisis of 1907. Not for nothing was it often remarked that the ghosts of the "Modernists" were looking over the shoulders of the conciliar fathers at the Second Vatican Council. The ideals for which Fogazzaro, von Hügel, Loisy, and Tyrrell had fought are no longer to be regarded as "out of date" and hence negligible; they are of vital importance for the Roman Catholic church and its relations to the rest of Christianity.[36]

Along with recognition of the merits of Fogazzaro's religious ideals comes a realization that his thinking and writing on the relation between science and religion cannot be dismissed as lightly as has been done heretofore. The great Catholic anthropologist Father Teilhard de Chardin[37] set forth, on the basis of his extensive professional competence in both physical anthropology and theology, opinions concerning evolution which were very close to those of Fogazzaro. The latter was, indeed, not a professional in either anthropology and biology or theology; but, far from deserving condemnation as a mere dilettante, he should be praised for the genius with which he anticipated the approach and findings of Teilhard de Chardin.

Once the prejudices which we have been discussing are set aside, it is not hard to see the message which Fogazzaro had for the Italy of his and later times. He urged:

(A) the need for a profound conversion, on the part of both clergy and laymen, to a closer approximation to true Christianity, remaining within the Roman church;

(B) the desirability of interpreting the Holy Scriptures and the dogmas of the Roman church in such a way as to abandon intellectual rigidity and narrowness for a recognition of the import of modern scientific discoveries;

(C) the necessity of applying a sense of morality, based upon Christian teachings but independent of Church organization, to public and especially political life, and also to private life, particularly in sexual matters;

(D) the value of foreign culture, literature, and music, regarded from an international rather than a strictly national point of view.

In Fogazzaro's own time, it was not wholly unrealistic for a writer to advocate ideas such as these. During and after the First World War and the Fascist period, Fogazzaro's ideals did indeed seem to recede farther and farther into the past. Since the defeat of Fascism, however, and since the Second Vatican Council, they no longer seem unrealistic. His writings, far from being mere period-pieces, have reacquired meaning for present-day Italy.

III   *Fogazzaro's Place in Italian Literature*

After the appearance of *Piccolo mondo antico*, Fogazzaro was widely regarded as the greatest Italian novelist since Manzoni. As we have seen, this opinion was replaced, after his death, by a much lower evaluation, classing him well below, say, Verga or Svevo. The pendulum now seems to be swinging in the opposite direction; several recent discussions[38] show that his work is regaining critical favor. It would seem reasonable to consider Fogazzaro simply as one of the leading writers of the second half of the nineteenth century, together with Nievo and Verga in prose and with Pàscoli and Carducci in poetry. His position relative to d'Annunzio will depend on the reader's or critic's evaluation of the merits of the latter. No single novelist, among those just mentioned or others, can be considered as having given a total picture of all the Italian life of his time, nor is it reasonable to expect such a portrayal from any one author. Each writer can present validly only what he knows from his own experience. As for Fogazzaro, it is not an exaggeration to say that he is unsurpassed in the picture that he gives of North Italian life—especially, but not exclusively, that of the upper-middle and lower-upper classes—of the late nineteenth century, a picture rich in humor, emotion, and psychological penetration, with a style exactly appropriate to his aims. The cultural symbolism of *Un'idea di Ermes Torranza*—that of an "old fogey" who brings separated people back together after his death—may yet prove to have been justified.

Notes and References

Preface

1. See Giuseppe Malagòli, *L'accentazione italiana* (Firenze, 1946).
2. As I have urged in my article "To Hyphenate or Not to Hyphenate," *English Journal*, LIII (1964), 662 - 665.

Chapter One

1. In Italian, the title *Don* is normally used with the given name, the family-name, or both, of a priest: e.g., *Don Giuseppe, Don Fogazzaro,* or *Don Giuseppe Fogazzaro. Don* and *Donna* can also be used (as are their Spanish equivalents *Don* and *Doña*) before the given names of upper-class persons—e.g., *Don Franco, Donna Fedele*—but nowadays this custom is continued only in southern Italy.

2. Antonio Rosmini-Serbati (1797 - 1855) was a leading Italian churchman and philosopher. Although desirous of seeing the resurgent Italian nation led by the pope, he was strongly critical of the faults of the church. His *Delle cinque piaghe della santa Chiesa* ("Of the Five Wounds of the Holy Church," 1848; English translation, 1883) was placed on the Index Expurgatorius in 1849.

3. T. Gallarati-Scotti, *La vita di Antonio Fogazzaro* (3rd ed., Milan, 1963), pp. 13 - 17.

4. *Ibid.*, pp. 17 - 19.

5. Giàcomo Zanella (1820 - 1888) is remembered chiefly for his poem *La conchiglia fòssile* ("The Fossil Conch-Shell"), a poetical presentation of the idea of human progress which has often been compared to Longfellow's *The Chambered Nautilus*.

6. All Fogazzaro's biographers cite an unpublished autobiographical memoir in which he speaks of the extent to which he despised himself for his weakness, passing many hours in sadness and depression. See Gallarati-Scotti, *Fogazzaro*, pp. 31 - 32.

7. Arrigo Boito (1842 - 1918) composed two operas, *Mefistòfele* and *Nerone* (the latter not performed until 1924), and wrote the libretti for Verdi's *Otello* (1887) and *Falstaff* (1893).

8. Gallarati-Scotti, *Fogazzaro*, p. 40.

9. D. and L. Piccioni, *Antonio Fogazzaro* (Turin, 1970), p. 140.

10. Especially by Lucienne Portier, *Antonio Fogazzaro* (Paris, 1937), Chapter 1, "La Nature."

11. L. Portier, *Fogazzaro*, pp. 34 - 38.

12. For instance, L. Portier, *Fogazzaro,* Chapter 1; Gallarati-Scotti, *Fogazzaro,* pp. 60 - 64; Piccioni, *Fogazzaro,* pp. 142 - 145; Piero Nardi, *Antonio Fogazzaro* (3rd ed., Milan, 1945), pp. 125 - 131.

Chapter Two

1. Piccioni, *Fogazzaro,* p. 132.

2. In the preface to *Miranda,* Fogazzaro explains that he wrote it to illustrate the possibility of one soul affecting another, even at a distance.

3. This relation between the success of *Miranda* and the *Zeitgeist* of immediately post-Risorgimento Italy is discussed more extensively by Gallarati-Scotti, *Fogazzaro,* pp. 55 - 57.

4. This has made it easy for his biographers to include pictures of various of his friends who served as models for one character or another in his stories.

5. For the general theory of the way in which a work of literature can present symbolically the various aspects of the culture out of which it grew, see R. A. Hall, Jr., *Cultural Symbolism in Literature* (Ithaca, N.Y., 1963).

6. Nardi, *Fogazzaro,* pp. 51 - 52.

7. Piccioni, *Fogazzaro,* pp. 121 - 122.

8. For a picture of the "Pliniana," see Nardi, *Fogazzaro,* opposite p. 193.

9. As done, for instance by A. Pompeati, *Letteratura italiana* (Turin, 1944 - 1950), pp. 517 - 522.

10. Beginning with the famous outburst which Dante puts in the mouth of the troubadour Sordello (*Purgatorio,* VI, 76 - 78):

Ahi serva Italia, di dolore ostello,
    nave sanza nocchiere in gran tempesta,
    non donna di provincie, ma bordello!

"Alas, enslaved Italy, dwelling-place of sorrow, ship without a helmsman in a great storm, not [any longer] the mistress of provinces, but [now] a harlot!" See also my discussion in R. A. Hall, Jr., *A Short History of Italian Literature* (Ithaca, N.Y., 1951), pp. 90 - 91.

11. Nardi, *Fogazzaro,* p. 15.

Chapter Three

1. Most of Fogazzaro's biographers—e.g., Gallarati-Scotti, *Fogazzaro,* p. 97; Nardi, *Fogazzaro,* p. 171; Piccioni, *Fogazzaro,* p. 166—quote Verga's letter of praise to Fogazzaro.

2. His original intention was to call it simply *Cortis,* the hero's family-name; only towards the end of his work on it did he change the title to *Daniele Cortis.*

3. His wife Rita was quite secure in the knowledge that her husband would not be physically unfaithful; she once told Felicitas Buchner "I am

not jealous of flesh-and-blood women, but only of my husband's heroines"
(Nardi, *Fogazzaro*, p. 392).

4. He planned to collect his poems for Felicitas in a book to be called *Il libro dell'amore immortale* "The Book of Immortal Love," but it was never published as such in his life-time. The poems intended for this collection were brought together by Nardi in Volume XI of his edition of Fogazzaro's complete works (Milan, 1939 - 40).

5. His letters to Felicitas are one of our major sources of information for his inner development from 1883 onwards.

6. From Pergolesi's *L'Olimpiade* (1735), to words by Metastasio:

Se cerca, se dice	"If she seeks, if she asks
L'amico dov'è?	'Where is my friend?'
L'amico infelice,	'The unhappy friend,'
Rispondi, morì.	Answer, 'died.'
Ah no, sì gran duolo	Ah, no, such great sorrow
Non darle per me;	Do not cause her on my account;
Rispondi, ma solo:	Answer, but only:
Piangendo, partì.	'Weeping, he departed.' "

7. Rome was taken on September 20, 1870; the capital was transferred from Florence to Rome in 1871.

8. See J. A. Thayer, *Italy and the Great War: Politics and Culture, 1870 - 1915* (Madison and Milwaukee, 1964), Chapter 3, "Parliament in Theory and Practice."

9. Taking its name from the Guelfs, mediaeval supporters of the papacy.

10. For instance, Luigi Tosti, abbot of Monte Cassino and an historian of the church; see Thayer, *Italy and the Great War*, p. 5.

11. Thayer, *ibid.*, p. 43.

12. As recognized by all historians of Italy, e.g., Denis Mack Smith, *Italy* (Ann Arbor, 1959), pp. 39 - 75.

13. This attitude is still wide-spread, and is often expressed by North Italians, whose dislike of the *meridionali* or southerners has been increased by post-Second-World-War mass migrations from the south into the industrial cities of the North.

14. Thayer, *Italy and the Great War*, pp. 113 - 121.

15. S. Jacini, *Storia del Partito Popolare Italiano* (Milan, 1951), pp. 4 - 5.

16. Quoted by Piccioni, *Fogazzaro*, pp. 191 - 193.

17. Such as Luigi Russo, in "Maestri e seguaci di Antonio Fogazzaro," *Belfagor*, X (1955), pp. 609 - 622.

18. Piccioni, *Fogazzaro*, p. 194.

19. *Belfagor*, X (1960), p. 612.

20. History proved Fogazzaro right in regard to Italy on at least two crucial occasions, when King Victor Emanuel III was too weak to keep Salandra from dragging Italy into the First World War in 1915 (cf. Thayer, *Italy and the Great War*, Chapter 1) and to keep Mussolini from seizing

power in 1922 (cf. Mack Smith, *Italy*, Chapter 44)—both of which events he could have prevented, had he possessed a minimum of courage and strength of character.

21. This episode may have been suggested by a similar event at the outset of Bismarck's parliamentary career; see Alan Palmer, *Bismarck* (New York, 1976), p. 33.

22. Piccioni, *Fogazzaro*, p. 211.

23. Attilio Momigliano, *Studî di poesia* (Bari, 1948), p. 231.

24. Piccioni, *Fogazzaro*, pp. 201 - 202.

25. For instance, *Ascensioni umane* (Milan, 1899).

26. "Di un carattere della più recente letteratura italiana," *La Critica*, V (1907), 177 - 190.

27. Matthew 22:30.

28. Reproduced by Nardi, *Fogazzaro*, opposite p. 304.

29. Visible in the photograph reproduced by Nardi, *Fogazzaro*, opposite p. 256.

30. Interestingly, Fogazzaro's two "practical" heroes, Daniele Cortis and Piero Maironi, know little or nothing about music. See our discussion in Chapter 8.

31. In this, his situation is similar to that of the Roumanian architect and master-builder Manole, who, in ancient legend, learns that in order to complete the beautiful cathedral which he is building, he must sacrifice what he holds most dear, his wife Caplea, by letting her be buried alive in the wall of the building—a legend with obvious symbolism applying to any creative endeavor.

32. *The Lonely Crowd* (New York, 1950).

33. On the rôle of these and other men of letters in fomenting antidemocratic feeling, glorifying war and violence, and creating an atmosphere in which a small group of war-mongers were able to force Italy into the war in 1915, see Thayer, *Italy and the Great War*, especially pp. 134 - 142 and Chapter 12, "The War as a Cultural Crisis."

Chapter Four

1. Gallarati-Scotti, *Fogazzaro*, p. 9.

2. Piccioni, *Fogazzaro*, p. 203.

3. A variant of the name *Tobler*, a well-known Eichstätt family.

4. S. Englert, "Eichstätt in Fogazzaros 'Geheimnis des Dichters'," *Deutsche Illustrierte Rundschau*, June, 1928, pp. 74 - 75; Hans Baier, "Fremde entdecken Eichstätt," *Eichstätter Kurier*, Dec. 31, 1969 and Jan. 1, 1970.

5. The present writer had this experience in Eichstätt in 1970, recognizing the Rossmarkt from Fogazzaro's description.

6. The "Libro d'Enrico" in *Miranda* is quite critical of (presumably

Milanese) bohemianism. Contemporary political concerns, in the persons of Steinegge and Count Césare d'Ormengo and their respective attitudes, enter into *Malombra*, which also contains a certain amount of social criticism in Fogazzaro's unfavorable description of the Milanese upper bourgeois society with which Silla comes into contact in the latter part of the story.

7. Fogazzaro was not fond of Wagner. When he heard *Die Meistersinger* in Munich, he did not like it (Piccioni, *Fogazzaro*, p. 214). Here, the adverb *detestabilmente* modifies the verb *cantò*, and the narrator does not specifically indicate that he considered the piece itself "detestable."

8. Antonio Piromalli, in *Orientamenti culturali: letteratura italiana—I minori* (Milan, 1962). IV, p. 3012.

9. Set forth in his lecture *Le grand poète de l'avenir*, delivered in Paris in 1898.

Chapter Five

1. Fogazzaro always had a good enough sense of humor to be able to laugh at his own fancies. In *Schumann (dall'op. 68)*, he was also turning the tables on his critics—most of whom have discussed that story and his other *Versioni dalla mùsica* without knowing the music involved.

2. A childish mispronunciation of the name *Margherita* by which his grand-daughter Margherita Roi was called in her family.

3. Gallarati-Scotti, *Fogazzaro*, pp. 164 - 167.

4. The English translations of this and others of Fogazzaro's novels were given fanciful names, often with little or no relation to the Italian titles (see the Bibliography). I have tried to give English equivalents for the Italian names of the stories which should be both accurate and idiomatic renditions of the originals.

5. In the period between 1815 and 1860, when Lombardy and Venetia were still under Austrian rule, the conservatives who favored the status quo were called by the pejorative name *austriacanti* "pro-Austrian."

6. The *Isola Bella* ("Beautiful Island") is in the Lago Maggiore, offshore from Stresa.

7. Nardi (*Fogazzaro*, pp. 417 - 418) reproduces a letter from Fogazzaro to a friend, listing a number of the characters of the novel together with the real-life persons from whom they were drawn.

8. Nardi, *Fogazzaro*, p. 330.

9. Nardi, *ibid.*, pp. 340 - 349 and 418 - 420, with a detailed analysis of the real Luisa's letters to Antonio and extensive excerpts showing the close similarity between certain facets of her personality and those of the heroine of *Piccolo mondo antico*.

10. Piccioni, *Fogazzaro*, p. 290.

11. An extensive discussion of the idealization of the Risorgimento is given by Thayer, *Italy and the Great War*, Chapters 1 and 2.

12. In the watered-down, popularized accounts of the Risorgimento

taught in elementary schools, especially during the Fascist period, these conflicts were minimized, so that the public at large had (and still has) a very unclear picture of the real situation before 1870. For an extensive discussion, though rather pro-Garibaldian and anti-Cavourian, see D. Mack Smith, *Cavour and Garibaldi, 1860: A Study in Political Conflict* (Cambridge [Eng.], 1954; *Victor Emanuel, Cavour and the Risorgimento* (London and New York, 1971).

13.   For a long time, critics tended to treat *Leila* as a work separate from and only tenuously related to the three novels in which Franco and Piero Maironi appear as living persons. Only Nardi (*Fogazzaro,* p. 555) and Kenneth McKenzie ("Antonio Fogazzaro," *Yale Review,* New Series, I [1911], 119 - 128) have realized that *Leila* forms an essential part of the Maironi series; and only McKenzie recognized its function in discussing how the survivors could "pick up the pieces" after the rejection of Benedetto's ideals.

14.   This is an old tradition in Italy, beginning with Petrarch in his *Secretum;* see any history of Italian literature.

15.   A number of literary works reflect such cultural nostalgia—for instance, Edmond Rostand's *Cyrano de Bergerac* (1897), Noël Coward's *Cavalcade* (1931), or Clarence Day's books about his parents (*God and My Father,* 1932; *Life with Father,* 1935; *Life with Mother,* 1937)—as pointed out in R. A. Hall, Jr., *Cultural Symbolism in Literature* (Ithaca, N.Y., 1963), pp. 112 - 119.

16.   Ultraclerical critics objected to *Piccolo mondo antico* because they considered that Fogazzaro had presented Luisa, the strong-minded skeptic and rationalist, in too favorable a light as contrasted with the religious but superficially weaker Franco (Piccioni, *Fogazzaro,* p. 312).

17.   Piccioni, *Fogazzaro,* pp. 314 - 319.

18.   In pre-republican Italy, senators were named by the king, not elected.

19.   Nardi (*Fogazzaro,* Chapter 21, "Francesi a Vicenza") devotes a whole chapter to his French visitors, many of them illustrious men of letters.

20.   Gallarati-Scotti, *Fogazzaro,* pp. 307, 311.

21.   In the Euganean Hills, seven miles south-west of Padua.

22.   Piccioni, *Fogazzaro,* pp. 339 - 343.

23.   As pointed out by many critics, especially Bernard De Voto, *The World of Fiction* (Boston, 1950).

24.   These characteristics are very evident in Vincenzo Corcos' portrait of Yole Moschini Biaggini, reproduced by Nardi (*Fogazzaro,* opp. p. 481) and Piccioni (*Fogazzaro,* opp. p. 176).

25.   Piccioni, *Fogazzaro,* p. 344.

26.   P. Nardi, *Fogazzaro su documenti inediti* (Vicenza, 1938), pp. 20 - 27.

27.   After Yole's early death in 1905, Fogazzaro visited her tomb and

wrote the poem *Nel cimitero di Pàdova* ("In the Cemetery of Padua") expressing his regret at not having been able to revive her Christian faith. This poem, published in the *Rassegna Nazionale* of December 1, 1905, was misinterpreted by many as a posthumous declaration of love on Fogazzaro's part.

28. As pointed out by Piccioni, *Fogazzaro*, pp. 353 - 354.
29. Nardi, *Fogazzaro*, pp. 521 - 522.
30. Piccioni, *Fogazzaro*, p. 353.
31. Represented in literature by the Umbrian poet Jacopone da Todi (1230 - 1306), the author of many *laude* or "songs of praise."
32. If, by chance, one's first contact with a series is with the second book rather than the first, one usually feels the same kind of let-down on later reading the first

Chapter Six

1. Nardi, Fogazzaro, pp. 225 - 226.
2. Baron Friedrich von Hügel (1852 - 1925) was born in Florence, and moved to England in 1867. Presumably he was a trilingual native speaker of German, Italian, and English.
3. Alfred Firmin Loisy (1857 - 1940), the author of a number of works on the gospels.
4. George Tyrrell (1861 - 1909), who entered the Roman Catholic church as a convert in 1879 and joined the Jesuits in 1880. After the unauthorized publication of his "Letter to a Professor of Anthropology," in an Italian translation, in the Milanese newspaper *Corriere della Sera* in January, 1906, Tyrrell was expelled from the Jesuit order in February of that year.
5. Don Ròmolo Murri (1870 - 1944) was a leader in the movement for participation of liberal Catholics in political and social matters, and founder of a movement with the name *democrazia cristiana* "Christian democracy," a blend of Neo-Thomism and socialism.
6. A. L. Lilley's *Modernism: A Record and Review* (London, 1908), a collection of magazine articles that appeared during the controversies, gives a contemporary English view of their development. See also Pietro Scòppola's *Crisi modernista e rinnovamento cattòlico* (Bologna, 1961; 2nd ed., 1969).
7. Piccioni, *Fogazzaro*, pp. 364 - 370.
8. Also known as the *Index Librorum Prohibitorum* ("Index of Prohibited Books"), this list was a catalogue of books which Catholics were forbidden to read without special permission from an ecclesiastical authority, because their faith might be damaged by the contents of the books. Established in the sixteenth century, the Index ceased to have binding force in 1966.
9. Scòppola, *Crisi modernista*, pp. 185 - 196.

10. A relatively inaccessible town in the valley of the Aniene, in the Apennines about thirty miles east of Rome as the crow flies.

11. About seven miles up the valley of the Aniene from Subiaco.

12. Nardi, *Fogazzaro*, pp. 556, 578.

13. His critics objected that Benedetto did not deserve the title of "saint" either through his own character or through having received official sanctification.

14. Matthew 19:21.

15. Piccioni, *Fogazzaro*, pp. 382 - 383.

16. Fuller discussion in R. A. Hall, Jr., "Fogazzaro's *Il santo* and Hochhuth's *Der Stellvertreter*," *Italian Quarterly*, X (1966), nos. 36/37, 22 - 33.

17. Extensive discussions of the rights and wrongs of Hochhuth's accusations can be found in Fritz J. Raddatz (ed.): *Summa Iniuria, oder durfte der Papst schweigen?* (Hamburg, 1963); Eric Bentley (ed.), *The Storm over* The Deputy (New York, 1964).

18. See the stage-directions for *Der Stellvertreter*, instructing the actor playing the rôle of Pacelli how to behave.

19. Nardi, *Fogazzaro*, pp. 570 - 583; Piccioni, *Fogazzaro*, pp. 389 -403.

20. Gallarati-Scotti, *Fogazzaro*, Chapter 19 ("La parola di Don Giuseppe Flores"); Nardi, *Fogazzaro*, Chapter 20 ("Nel fumo della battaglia"); Piccioni, *Fogazzaro*, pp. 424 - 429.

21. Reproduced in Gallarati-Scotti (to whose care it was entrusted), *Fogazzaro*, pp. 471 - 478.

22. The definitive edition, with extensive bibliography, appeared in 1912.

23. A small town at the south end of Lake Lugano, where passengers change from train to boat.

24. Piccioni, *Fogazzaro*, p. 453.

25. By chance, the writer stayed at this hotel on his first visit to Milan in 1930.

Chapter Seven

1. Raffaele Viola, *Fogazzaro* (Florence, 1939), pp. 1 - 38.

2. Lucienne Portier (*Fogazzaro*, pp. 93 - 94) remarks: "All that [the pride and sensitivity of Lelia and Marcello] yields to their triumphant love and ends in a marriage—nothing more simple, more normal, more 'orderly': love in marriage."

3. As pointed out by many critics, and discussed in detail by Mlle. Portier (*Fogazzaro*, Part IV, Chapter VI, "La représentation de la mort").

4. Piero Giacosa, *Antonio Fogazzaro: commemorazione* (Milan, 1911), p. 15.

5. Piccioni, *Fogazzaro*, p. 149.

6. Discussed in detail by Portier, *Fogazzaro*, pp. 409 - 412.

7.   This aspect of Fogazzaro's work is discussed extensively by Giorgio de Rienzo, *Fogazzaro e l'esperienza della realtà* (Milan, 1967).

8.   Thorough discussion in de Rienzo, *Fogazzaro e l'esperienza della realtà*, Chapter 2 ("La quieta giornata della villa fogazzariana").

9.   In Italian, this word refers to any building of considerable size, not necessarily a "palace" in the English sense.

10.   *Fogazzaro e l'esperienza della realtà*, Chapter I ("Il 'verticalismo' nello spazio e nel tempo").

11.   Among authors of high literary reputation, we may mention Franz Kafka who had no hesitation in writing his *Amerika* with absolutely no first-hand experience. The list could be extended downward almost indefinitely, ending with Karl May and his numberless stories about American Indians, and numerous contemporary writers of novels about the Second World War.

12.   See de Rienzo, *Fogazzaro e l'esperienza della realtà*, pp. 56 - 58, note 37.

13.   This is why Fogazzaro's narrative technique, so often compared to that of the "realistic" school of novelists (e.g., Verga or Capuana in Italy, Flaubert or Maupassant in France), is fundamentally different from theirs. He learned far more from his reading of the American novelist William Dean Howells (1837 - 1920) than from the French or Italian realists. The Piccionis (*Fogazzaro*, p. 282) are the first of his biographers or critics to take this into account.

14.   An expression in one of Horace's odes (Book I, no. 4, vv.16 - 17) which may mean either "and fables [and] shades of the dead" or "shades of the dead of fable," depending on whether *fabulae* is taken as nominative plural or genitive singular.

15.   Extensive discussion of this and other "farewells" in de Rienzo, *Fogazzaro e l'esperienza della realtà*, pp. 58 - 60.

16.   See my *The Comic Style of P. G. Wodehouse* (Hamden, Connecticut, 1974), pp. 53, 75-76.

17.   As pointed out by de Rienzo, *Fogazzaro e l'esperienza della realtà*, throughout.

Chapter Eight

1.   For a full discussion of the rôle played by music in Fogazzaro's works, see my "Music in the Works of Fogazzaro," in W. W. Austin (ed.), *New Looks at Italian Opera—Essays in Honor of Donald J. Grout* (Ithaca, N.Y., 1968), pp. 220 - 259; Italian translation, *La mùsica nelle òpere di Antonio Fogazzaro* (Florence, 1968).

2.   The fifth is a passage in *Piccolo mondo moderno* where Carlino Dessalle, a basically unsympathetic character, makes unfavorable remarks about Mendelssohn.

3.   Fogazzaro's neglect of the opera as an all-pervasive phenomenon in

Italian public musical life seems to have been repaid by operatic composers' neglect of his works. The only opera derived from one of Fogazzaro's works is, as far as I know, Franco Alfano's *Miranda* (1896).

4. For detailed analysis of the twenty-eight passages which I have classified as "longer episodes," see pp. 230 - 253 of my article "Music in the Works of Fogazzaro" (note 1 to this chapter).

5. For the relation of the structure of music to that of language, see my article "La struttura della mùsica e del linguaggio," *Nuova Rivista Musicale Italiana*, VII (1973), 206 - 225.

6. In "Language and Tradition"—in D. Daiches and A. Thorlby (eds.), *Literature and Western Civilization* (London, 1976), VI, 177 - 198—I have attempted to give a comparative morphology of the development of European and American standard languages since the mid-eighteenth century.

7. For this reason, a great deal of the flavor of Twain's style is lost in translations of *Huck Finn*, almost all of which use only the standard language to render Huck's narration and the speech of the other characters.

8. Manzoni lived in Florence for two months in 1827 to "rinse out his language in the Arno." In some instances, he went too far because the modern language has in fact taken up some Lombardisms which he rejected. For instance, he replaced the Lombard term *robiola* "a kind of cheese" by the Tuscan *raveggiolo*. In the mid-twentieth century, however, that kind of cheese has become known throughout Italy (including Tuscany) by the Lombard name *robiolina* (with the diminutive suffix *-ina*). The Tuscan word *raveggiolo* is unknown to present-day readers of Manzoni so that it has be to glossed with the Lombard word which he had rejected. See M. Medici, "*Robiola* e *raveggiolo*," *Lingua Nostra*, XIX (1958), 93 - 94.

9. In his *Il diavolo del Sant'Ufficio* ("The Devil of the Holy Office," 1847), Antonio Zanolini had made use of Bolognese dialect, as pointed out by G. F. Contini in "Un paragrafo sconosciuto della storia dell'italiano letterario nell'Ottocento," in *Überlieferung und Gestaltung: Festgabe für Theophil Spoerri* (Zürich, 1950), pp. 127 - 140; but this was an exception, passed over in even the most detailed histories of Italian literature.

10. Literally, "Tuscan gargling"—the pronunciation of single /k/ between vowels as *h*, for instance *la casa* "the house" as *la hasa*, or *la chiesa* "the church" as *la hiesa*.

11. Attested, for example, on map 369 of K. Jaberg and J. Jud, *Sprach- und Sachatlas Italiens und der Südschweiz* (Zofingen, 1928 - 40).

12. Used in this sense by the poet Ugo Fóscolo (1778 - 1827); cf. C. Battisti and G. Alessio, *Dizionario Etimologico Italiano* (Florence, 1950 - 57), II, 848.

13. For instance, by G. Trombatore in his *Fogazzaro* (Messina and Milan, 1938) and in the (largely erroneous) criticisms of A. Piromalli in the

chapter "La critica del realismo e della musicalità" of his *Fogazzaro e la critica* (Florence, 1952).

14. Especially in his two fundamental articles, "Criteria for Style Analysis," *Word*, XV (1959), 154 - 174, and "Stylistic Context," *Word*, XVI (1960), 207 - 218.

15. I am following the distinction made by John S. Kenyon—in his article "Cultural Levels and Functional Varieties of English," *College English*, X (1948), 31 - 36; reprinted in Harold B. Allen (ed.), *Applied English Linguistics* (New York, 1958), pp. 215 - 221—between standard and non-standard, formal and informal, and the four-way contrast resulting from the possible combinations of these two cultural levels and two functional varieties.

16. For an exemplification of these principles, see my *The Comic Style of P. G. Wodehouse* (Hamden, Connecticut, 1974).

17. For the relation between poetry and linguistic structure, see especially Edward Sapir, *Language* (New York, 1921), Chapter XI ("Language and Literature"); Charles F. Hockett, *A Course in Modern Linguistics* (New York, 1958), Chapter 63 ("Literature"), particularly section 63.4 ("Prose and Poetry"); Robert A. Hall, Jr., *Introductory Linguistics* (Philadelphia, 1964), Chapter 69 ("Linguistics and Literature").

18. Ulrich Leo, in his excellent *Fogazzaros Stil und der symbolistische Lebensroman* (Heidelberg, 1928), is concerned primarily with the themes and topics of Fogazzaro's work—especially in *Malombra* and *Leila*—rather than with the specifically linguistic features of his style.

19. "The position of the adverb in English—a convenient analogy to the position of the adjective in Spanish," *Hispania*, XXVI (1943), 191 - 192; "Adjective position again," *Hispania*, LV (1972), 91 - 94.

20. There are also twenty-eight or fifteen and one-tenth percent, which are followed by phrases introduced by prepositions, and four nouns, or two and one-tenth percent, followed by adjectival clauses. These two kinds of modifiers, however, can only come after the noun in Italian, and therefore their position conveys no information as to contrast or the absence thereof.

21. Fogazzaro's contemporary Gabriele d'Annunzio (1863 - 1938) is reported—e.g. by the Piccionis, *Fogazzaro*, p. 51—to have called Fogazzaro's style *un linguaggio da capostazione* "a station-master's way of using language." This somewhat Sybilline utterance perhaps refers to Fogazzaro's sobriety and directness in his imagery, in contrast to the type of pretentious and high-flown rhetoric with which d'Annunzio bedecked his writings.

22. Maria Luisa Summer's "Le approssimazioni stilìstiche di Antonio Fogazzaro," in *Giornale Storico della Letteratura Italiana*, CXXXVIII (1961), 402 - 442, 522 - 551, is the only extensive study of Fogazzaro's style to have been published to date in Italy. Unfortunately, it is marked by

almost total incomprehension of Fogazzaro's aims and consequent mis-representation of his achievement. A new, full study is called for, perhaps with some title like "Le esattezze stilìstiche di A. F."

23. As pointed out by de Rienzo, *Fogazzaro e l'esperienza della realtà*, pp. 230 - 231.

Chapter Nine

1. Ippòlito Nievo (1832 - 1861) was the author of *Le Confessioni di un Italiano* (written 1857 - 58, published posthumously in 1867), a long historical novel of the Risorgimento, highly esteemed by critics and readers alike.

2. See especially Pietro Scòppola, *Crisi modernista e rinnovamento cattòlico in Italia* (Bologna, 1961).

3. Emilio Scampini, *L'arte di Fogazzaro* (Florence, 1962).

4. In his article "Di un caràttere della più recente letteratura italiana," in *La Critica*, V (1907), 177 - 190; with some modifications in the section "Antonio Fogazzaro" of his *La letteratura della nuova Italia* (Bari, 1914), IV, 129 - 140.

5. See B. Croce, *Estetica come scienza dell'espressione e linguistica generale* (Milan, 1902). With such narrow criteria as these, the Old French *Chanson de Roland*, Milton's *Paradise Lost*, or Ibsen's *Ghosts* and *An Enemy of the People* would stand condemned for their political, religious, or social content!

6. The principal Crocean critics of Fogazzaro have been Francesco Flora, in his *Storia della letteratura italiana* (Milan, 1940); Attilio Momigliano, *Studî di poesia* (second edition, Bari, 1948) and *Storia della letteratura italiana* (eighth edition, Milan and Messina, 1956); Luigi Russo, in several articles in his journal *Belfagor* (see Selected Bibliography), gathered together in his *Il tramonto del letterato* (Bari, 1960); and such authors of school-texts as Aurelia Accame Bobbio, *Profilo stòrico della letteratura italiana* (Brescia, 1963).

7. The chief "ex-fan" critics have been Eugenio Donadoni, Antonio Piromalli, and Raffaello Viola; see the Selected Bibliography.

8. For Fogazzaro's attitude towards socialism, see Piccioni, *Fogazzaro*, pp. 333 - 335.

9. An exception was a certain G. P. Lucini, whose criticisms of Fogazzaro have been reprinted by E. Ghidetti, in *Le idee e le virtù di Antonio Fogazzaro* (Padua, 1974), pp. 35 - 102.

10. In his *Fogazzaro e la crìtica* (Florence, 1951), and *Fogazzaro* (Palermo, 1959).

11. From a Crocean position in Fascist days, expressed in his *Fogazzaro* (Milan and Messina, 1939), Trombatore passed to a Marxist type of criticism in his "Il successo di Fogazzaro," *Risorgimento*, I (1945), 442 -455 (reprinted in *Belfagor*, X [1955], 138 - 149).

12. *Miti e coscienza del decadentismo italiano* (Milan, 1960).

13. A judgment based clearly on *Piccolo mondo antico* alone, since all of Fogazzaro's other books are strongly future-oriented.

14. *Fogazzaro*, pp. 20 - 26.

15. Nor would the allegation that Jeanne and Noemi were "subconsciously homosexual," as some have suggested, be anything but a *petitio principii*. In Freudian analysis, the "subconscious" is all too often simply a means of begging the question, a device to assume as already demonstrated that which it is intended to demonstrate.

16. Francesco Flora, *Storia della letteratura italiana* (Milan, 1940).

17. Charles Baudelaire (1821 - 1867), translator of Edgar Allan Poe into French and author of the poems contained in the collection *Les fleurs du mal* (1857).

18. Filippo Marinetti (1878 - 1947), the leader of the "futurist" movement in France and Italy in the early twentieth century.

19. Aldo Palazzeschi (1885 - 1975), the author of many futurist and surralistic novels and short stories.

20. A widely told joke, after the Mass was ordered to be said in Italian, was that of the man who preferred to hear it in Latin: "As long as it was in Latin, I didn't understand it; but now that it's in Italian, it seems to me like a lot of balderdash."

21. Giosuè Carducci (1835 - 1904), a professor of classical literature at the University of Bologna and the author of much classically inspired poetry.

22. See Taylor, *Italy and the Great War*, pp. 192 - 205.

23. Alberto Moravia, pseudonym of Alberto Pincherle (1907 -   ), author of *Gl'indifferenti* ("The Indifferent Ones") and many other novels and short stories of Roman life, cold and unfeeling.

24. Ìtalo Svevo, pseudonym of Èttore Schmitz (1861 - 1928), of Trieste, author of several psychoanalytically oriented novels. His work and style have often been condemned because, as a Triestine, he was not purely Italian (his father was Austrian), and his language and style have been criticized because they reflected Triestine rather than purely Tuscan usage.

25. For Renaissance literary criticism, see especially Bernard Weinberg: *A History of Literary Criticism in the Italian Renaissance* (Chicago, 1961) and Baxter Hathaway, *The Age of Criticism: The Late Renaissance in Italy* (Ithaca, N.Y., 1962).

26. For Croce's doctrines with regard to literature, a good though somewhat uncritical discussion will be found in G. W. G. Orsini's *Benedetto Croce, Philosopher of Art and Literary Critic* (Carbondale, Illinois, 1961); see also A. H. Gilbert, "Benedetto Croce's Poetic," *Italica*, XLI (1964), 150 - 157.

27. In his obituary notice of Fogazzaro, in the *Yale Review*, New Series, I (1911), 119 - 128.

28. In her *Antonio Fogazzaro* (Paris, 1928).

29. In his *Fogazzaros Stil und der symbolistische Lebensroman* (Heidelberg, 1928).

30. "Fogazzaro nach fünfzig Jahren," in his *Philologische Schatzgräbereien* (München, 1968), pp. 391 - 402.

31. Thus L. Russo in his *Il tramonto del letterato* (Bari, 1960).

32. For the term *decadent* and its definitions, see Riccardo Scrivano, "Storia crìtica di un concetto letterario: decadentismo," in *Rassegna della Letteratura Italiana*, LXV (1961), 418 - 452; *Il decadentismo e la crìtica* (Florence, 1963).

33. Thus, for instance, A. Accame-Bobbio in her *Profilo stòrico della letteratura italiana* (Brescia, 1963).

34. Edoardo de Amicis (1846 - 1908), the author of the sentimental but widely read *Cuore* (1886), various short stories, and *L'idioma gentile* (1905), a defense of Manzoni's theories on the Italian standard language.

35. Luigi Capuana (1839 - 1915), a follower of the extreme realistic school, and the author of *Il marchese di Roccaverdina* (1901) and other novels.

36. As observed by Rheinfelder, a serious and devout German Catholic (note 30 to this chapter).

37. Pierre Teilhard de Chardin (1881 - 1955), Catholic priest, palaeontologist, and exponent of a synthesis of science and Christianity, especially in his *Le phénomène humain* (1947, published posthumously in 1955; Eng. tr., *The Phenomenon of Man*, 1959) and *Le milieu divin* (1957; Eng. tr., *The Divine Milieu*, 1960).

38. Especially the books of de Rienzo, Scampini, and the Piccionis, cited frequently in these notes; see the Selected Bibliography.

Selected Bibliography

PRIMARY SOURCES

Dell'avvenire del romanzo in Italia. Discorso. Vicenza: Burato, 1872.

Miranda. Firenze: Le Monnier, 1874.

Valsolda. Milano: Brìgola, 1876.

Malombra. Romanzo. Milano: Brìgola, 1881. Eng. tr., London: Unwin, 1896; reissued under title *The Woman*, 1907.

Daniele Cortis. Romanzo. Torino: Casanova, 1885. Three English translations: by Mrs. I. R. Tilton, New York: Holt, 1887; by S. L. Simeon, London: Remington, 1890; by G. Mantellini, *The Politician*, New York: Luce, 1908.

Eden Anto. In *Fanfulla della Domenica*, Nov. 8, 1885. Eng. tr., San Francisco: The Roxburghe Club, 1930.

Un'opinione di Alessandro Manzoni. Discorso. Firenze: Cellini, 1887.

Fedele ed altri racconti. [Short stories.] Milano: Galli, 1887.

Il mistero del poeta. Romanzo. Milano: Galli, 1888. Eng. tr., *The Poet's Mystery*, London: Duckworth, 1893.

Per la bellezza di un'idea. In *La Rassegna Nazionale* (Firenze), September 1, 1892.

Racconti brevi. [Short stories.] Roma: Voghera, 1894.

Piccolo mondo antico. Romanzo. Milano: Galli, 1895. Eng. tr., *The Patriot*, London: Hodder and Stoughton, and New York: Holt, 1906.

Poesie scelte. [Selected poems.] Milano: Galli, 1898.

Discorsi. Milano: Cogliati, 1898.

Ascensioni umane. Milano: Baldini e Castoldi, 1899.

Piccolo mondo moderno. Romanzo. Milano: Hoepli, 1901. Eng. tr., *The Man of the World*, London: Putnam, 1906 (issued in New York under title *The Sinner*).

Minime. Studî, discorsi e nuove lìriche. Milano: Aliprandi, 1901.

Idillii spezzati. Racconti brevi. [Short stories.] Milano: Baldini e Castoldi, 1901.

Il santo. Romanzo. Milano: Baldini e Castoldi, 1905. Eng. tr., *The Saint*, London: Hodder and Stoughton, 1906.

Le poesie. Milano: Baldini e Castoldi, 1908. French tr. by L. Portier, Paris: Boivin, 1937.

Leila. Romanzo. Milano: Baldini e Castoldi, 1910. Eng. tr., London, Hodder and Stoughton, 1911.

Tutte le òpere ("Complete Works") *di Antonio Fogazzaro*. Milano: Mondadori, 1930 - 45. Complete critical edition by Piero Nardi.

SECONDARY SOURCES

ATENE, PAOLO. *L'amore nelle òpere di A. Fogazzaro* ("Love in the Works of Antonio Fogazzaro"). Gènova: Libreria Editrice Italia, 1932. Criticism of Fogazzaro's treatment of love, by an ex-fan.

──── *Religione e misticismo in Antonio Fogazzaro* ("Religion and mysticism in Antonio Fogazzaro"). Torino: Paravia, 1934. Criticism of treatment of religion and mysticism.

BALDUCCI, ERNESTO. *Antonio Fogazzaro*. Brescia: Morcelliana, 1952. General treatment, from clerical point of view.

CABIBBE, GIORGIO. *Antonio Fogazzaro nel giudizio della critica* ("Antonio Fogazzaro in the Judgment of Criticism"). N.p., Istituto d'Alta Cultura, 1943. Survey of critical opinions with emphasis on negative aspect.

CROCE, BENEDETTO. "Di un carattere della più recente letteratura italiana" ("On a characteristic of the most recent Italian literature"). *La Critica*, V (1907), 177 - 190. Considers Fogazzaro insincere because of combination of eroticism and religiosity.

──── "Antonio Fogazzaro." In *La letteratura della nuova Italia* (Bari: Laterza, 1914), IV, 129 - 140. Repeats criticism of Fogazzaro's presumed "insincerity."

DE RIENZO, GIORGIO. *Fogazzaro e l'esperienza della realtà* ("Fogazzaro and the experience of reality"). Milano: Silva, 1967. Sympathetic study, analysing Fogazzaro's emphasis on depth rather than breadth of experience; the rôle of calm in the villa-oriented existence of Fogazzaro's characters; the nature of crimes in his stories and their relation to sickness and death; and the Fogazzarian novel as remembrance of intensely lived experience.

DONADONI, EUGENIO. *Antonio Fogazzaro*. Nàpoli: Perretta, 1913. Negative evaluation by an ex-fan.

FINCO, ALDO. "L'umorismo di Antonio Fogazzaro" ("The Humor of Antonio Fogazzaro"). *Romance Notes*, XV (1973/74), 522 - 526. Brief discussion of some of Fogazzaro's humorous passages.

FORTINI, ARMANDO (ed.). ("On the Fiftieth Anniversary of the Death of Antonio Fogazzaro") *Nel 50° anniversario della morte di Antonio Fogazzaro*. S. Marìa degli Àngeli, Assisi: Porziùncola, 1961. Collection of commemorative and evaluative essays.

GALLARATI-SCOTTI, TOMMASO. *La vita di Antonio Fogazzaro* ("The Life of Antonio Fogazzaro"). Milano: Mondadori, 1920. The "official" biography begun soon after Fogazzaro's death in 1911 by one of his last and most favorite disciples.

──── *La vita di Antonio Fogazzaro, dalle memorie e dai carteggi inèditi* ("The Life of Antonio Fogazzaro, based on unpublished memoirs and correspondence"). Milano: Mondadori, 1934. Second edition, 1963. Greatly amplified version of the 1920 biography; in the 1963 version, the definitive life of Fogazzaro with complete bibliography of his works.

GHIDETTI, ENRICO. *Le idee e le virtù di Antonio Fogazzaro* ("The Ideas and the Virtues of Antonio Fogazzaro"). Padova: Liviana, 1974. Leftist criticism of *Daniele Cortis*, pp. 1 - 33; discussion of criticism of Fogazzaro by early leftist critic G. P. Lucini, pp. 35 - 102.

HALL, ROBERT A., JR. "Fogazzaro's Maironi tetralogy." *Italica*, XLII (1965), no. 2, pp. 248 - 259. Emphasizes the unity of the four books dealing with the Maironi family (including *Leila*) and discusses their cultural symbolism.

_____. "Hochhuth's *Der Stellvertreter* and Fogazzaro's *Il santo*." *Italian Quarterly*, X (1967), nos. 36/37, pp. 22 - 33. Discusses the similarities and the differences between Fogazzaro's and Hochhuth's treatments of the same theme, the shortcomings of the Catholic church and criticisms of it from within.

_____. "The poet and his culture: Fogazzaro's *Miranda*." *Césare Barbieri Courier*, VIII (1967), no. 2, 20 - 22. Interpretation of cultural symbolism in *Miranda*.

_____. "Music in the works of Fogazzaro." In W. W. Austin (ed.): *New Looks at Italian Opera—Essays in Honor of Donald J. Grout* (Ithaca, N.Y.: 1967), pp. 220 - 259. Ital. tr.: *La mùsica nelle òpere di Antonio Fogazzaro*, Firenze: Gràfica Toscana, 1967. Extensive discussion, with detailed statistical analyses, of all passages in Fogazzaro's fiction involving music.

_____. *Antonio Fogazzaro e la crisi dell'Italia moderna. Saggio d'interpretazione letterario-morale* ("Antonio Fogazzaro and the Crisis of Modern Italy. An Essay in Literary-Moral Criticism"). Ithaca, N.Y.: Linguistica, 1967. Polemic defense of Fogazzaro's works and ideas against criticisms by clericals, Croceans, Marxists, and ex-fans.

_____. Review of G. de Rienzo, *Fogazzaro e l'esperienza della realtà*. *Italica*, XLVIII (1970), 218 - 220.

LEO, ULRICH. *Fogazzaros Stil und der symbolistische Lebensroman* ("Fogazzaro's Style and the Symbolic Biographic Novel"). Heidelberg, Winter, 1928. Sympathetic discussion of Fogazzaro's work, especially *Malombra* and *Leila*, from point of view of thematics and semantics rather than of stylistics in the narrow sense of the term.

MAYNIAL, ÉDOUARD. "De Stendhal à Fogazzaro: la poésie de la musique chez un écrivain italien" ("From Stendhal to Fogazzaro: the poetry of music in an Italian writer"). *Revue de Littérature Comparée*, XII (1933), 630 - 650. General discussion of music and its rôle in Fogazzaro's works.

McKENZIE, KENNETH. "Antonio Fogazzaro." *Yale Review*, New Series, I (1911), 119 - 128. Obituary article including extensive discussion and critical evaluation of Fogazzaro's achievement. The only critic to have perceived the true significance of *Leila* in relation to the three preceding novels.

MOLMENTI, POMPEO. *Antonio Fogazzaro: la sua vita e le sue òpere* ("Antonio Fogazzaro: his Life and Works"). Milano: Hoepli, 1900. An early biography written by an admirer while Fogazzaro was still alive.

MORRA, ANTONIO. *Fogazzaro nel suo piccolo mondo (dai carteggi famigliari* ("Fogazzaro in His Little World, from Intimate Correspondence"). Bologna: Cappelli, 1960. Primarily a collection of previously unpublished letters from and to Fogazzaro, casting light on previously unclear aspects of his life and work. As biography, somewhat uncritically admiring.

NARDI, PIERO. *Fogazzaro su documenti inèditi* ("Fogazzaro, from Unpublished Documents"). Vicenza: Jacchìa, 1930. Second edition, Vicenza: Jacchìa, 1938. Discussion of various aspects of Fogazzaro's life based on previously unpublished materials.

————. *Antonio Fogazzaro.* Milano: Mondadori, 1938. Second edition, 1941; third edition, 1945. The most extensive treatment of Fogazzaro from both a biographical and a critical point of view. In general favorable, though not naïvely or uncritically admiring. Very full chronology of Fogazzaro's writings, and discussion of critical studies of his work up to 1940.

PICCIONI, DONATELLA and LEONE. *Antonio Fogazzaro.* Torino: UTET, 1970. The only modern discussion of Fogazzaro, from both a critical and a biographical point of view, with a Catholic but not clerical orientation, and taking into account the changed atmosphere in Catholic thinking since the Second Vatican Council. Basically sympathetic, but not uncritical.

PICGIOLI, FERRUCCIO. *L'òpera letteraria di un mìstico: A. Fogazzaro* ("The Literary Work of a Mystic: A. Fogazzaro"). Torino: Paravia, 1930. Discussion primarily from the point of view of Fogazzaro's presumed self-confession and autobiography in his novels.

PIROMALLI, ANTONIO. *Fogazzaro e la crìtica* ("Fogazzaro and Criticism"). Firenze: La Nuova Italia, 1951. Detailed presentation and analysis of critical evaluations of Fogazzaro's work. Strongly negative position, with Marxist-based hostility compounded with ex-fan reaction.

————. *Fogazzaro.* Palermo: Palumbo, 1959. Over-all criticism, finding fault with Fogazzaro's religious, social, and artistic positions because they did not coïncide with Marxist theories of social development.

————. "Antonio Fogazzaro." In *Orientamenti culturali: letteratura italiana—I minori* (Milano: Marzorati, 1962), vol. IV, pp. 2987 -3057. Long article in leftist-oriented survey of Italian literature, attempting to "cut Fogazzaro down to size" by classifying him as "minor" and condemning his positions because of their non-conformity to Marxist dogma.

POMPEATI, ARTURO. "Antonio Fogazzaro e la mùsica" ("Antonio Fogazzaro and Music"). *Il Pianoforte*, VI (1915), 213 - 221.

PORTIER, LUCIENNE. *Antonio Fogazzaro*. Paris: Boivin, 1937. The most detailed critical study of Fogazzaro's subject-matter and technique. Views him primarily as a poet, and sees reflections of his essentially poetic approach in both his prose and his verse. Strongly sympathetic, without predetermined critical stance.

_____. "Un cinquantenaire ('A Fiftieth Anniversary'): Antonio Fogazzaro (1842 - 1911)." *Revue des Études Italiennes*, Nouvelle Série, VIII (1961), 179 - 184. Retrospective evaluation (positive) of Fogazzaro's work and its merits after fifty years.

RHEINFELDER, HANS. "Fogazzaro nach fünfzig Jahren" ("Fogazzaro after Fifty Years"). In Rheinfelder: *Philologische Schatzgräbereien* (München: Hueber, 1968), pp. 391 - 402. Retrospective evaluation, strongly favorable, especially from the religious point of view.

RUMOR, SEBASTIANO. *Antonio Fogazzaro*. Milano: Baldini e Castoldi, 1895. Second edition, Milano: Baldini e Castoldi, 1912. The first full biography, written by Fogazzaro's first major disciple. The second, definitive edition contains a very full bibliography of Fogazzaro's writings and of the obituaries and similar critical evaluations of his work that appeared immediately following his death. At present, valuable chiefly for bibliography; as biography, rather uncritically hagiographical, and replaced later by Gallarati-Scotti's and Nardi's books, which are based on much unpublished material (furnished especially by Felicitas Buchner) which was not available to Rumor.

_____. *Per Antonio Fogazzaro* ("For Antonio Fogazzaro"). Vicenza: Rumor, 1913 - 14; 2 vols. Collection of telegrams, articles, etc., commemorating Fogazzaro's death.

RUSSO, LUIGI. "Maestri e seguaci di Antonio Fogazzaro" ("Teachers and Followers of Antonio Fogazzaro"). *Belfagor*, X (1955), 609 - 622.

_____. "L'arte narrativa del Fogazzaro" ("The Narrative Art of Fogazzaro"). *Belfagor*, XI (1956), 22 - 36.

_____. "Il Fogazzaro nella storia" ("Fogazzaro in History"). *Belfagor*, XI (1956), 373 - 392.

_____. *Il tramonto del letterato* ("The Decline of the Man of Letters"). Bari: Laterza, 1960. Contains (pp. 282 - 336) a reworking of the three articles from *Belfagor* listed above. As a Sicilian, Russo was hostile to Fogazzaro, the North Italian; as a Crocean, to Fogazzaro, the mixer of the "poetic" with the "unpoetic"; and as a leftist, to Fogazzaro, the royalist, Catholic, and advocate of a "Christian democracy." His criticism is consequently motivated by strong animus, manifesting itself in harsh and often unsubstantiated judgments.

SALINARI, CARLO. *Miti e coscienza del decadentismo italiano* ("Myths and Conscience of Italian Decadentism"). Milano: Feltrinelli, 1960. Considers Fogazzaro to have been "decadent," and criticizes him for not having foreseen the future in Marxist terms.

SCAMPINI, EMILIO. *L'arte di Fogazzaro* ("Fogazzaro's Art"). Firenze: Cymba, 1962. Basically favorable study of Fogazzaro's achievements, but disapproving of the inclusion of "unpoetic" topics such a religion and politics.

SUMMER, MARIA LUISA. "Le approssimazioni stilistiche di Antonio Fogazzaro" ("The Stylistic Approximations of Antonio Fogazzaro"). *Giornale Stòrico della Letteratura Italiana*, CXXXVIII (1961), 402 - 442, 522 - 551. Strongly negative evaluation of Fogazzaro's themes, character-types, and use of dialect, from a Crocean point of view.

TROMBATORE, GAETANO. *Fogazzaro*. Milano e Massina: Principato, 1938. Negative criticism on Crocean basis.

————. "Il successo di Fogazzaro" ("Fogazzaro's Success"). *Risorgimento*, I (1945), 442 - 455; reprinted in *Belfagor*, X (1955), 138 - 149. Marxist condemnation of Fogazzaro as having achieved popularity through agreement with ideals of late nineteenth-century upper bourgeoisie.

VIOLA, RAFFAELLO. *Fogazzaro*. Firenze: Sansoni, 1939. Ex-fan, reacting against Fogazzaro's supposedly exclusive attention to emotion and autobiographical confession.

Index

153